PRAISE FOR EMAIL PERSUASION

"Email Persuasion is a great asset for any social media library. Ian brings a wealth of knowledge and practical experience to the fore. It's a must-read book and Ian ranks as one of the top international advisers in social media along with Chris Brogan, Mari Smith, and Amy Porterfield."

John Ashcroft, Chief Executive Pro-Manchester.

"The best thing about Ian's approach to e-mail marketing is that it works! We've seen a three-fold increase in leads and we've won several new clients for our consulting work, mostly without competition. Inspiring but practical. Ian certainly motivated me to get into action."

Adrian Willmott, Managing Direct⁺ cus (ng.

"If you have an⸱ doubts about the ⸱ efficacy ⸱ail marketing, thi⸱ ⸱ awa⸱ gives you ⸱⸱ deal on why e⸱ ⸱ew clients. ⸱⸱k full of detail⸱ ⸱⸱ p-by-step plan to create your o⸱ works!"

⸱rks Design.

"By page 5 t⸱ ⸱s over. To paraphrase Ia⸱ "⸱⸱ ⸱⸱ do i⸱⸱ ⸱ny one idea from this a⸱ ⸱lid c⸱ ⸱nse on email marketing, a⸱ ⸱⸱p⸱ ⸱⸱

⸱n ⸱⸱ **ified Coach.**

EMAIL
PERSUASION

IAN BRODIE

ISBN: 978-0-9927631-1-4

Published by Rainmaker Publishing

DEDICATION

It's traditional to dedicate your first book to your family, and I'm not going to buck that trend. If it hadn't been for the support, the understanding and sometimes a little gentle pushing from Kathy, Chris and Robs, then this book would never have seen the light of day.

CONTENTS

ACKNOWLEDGEMENTS · i

INTRODUCTION · iii
Why email is the world's most powerful marketing tool

1 WINNING CLIENTS WITH EMAIL · 1
The foundations of effective email marketing

2 SIGN ME UP · 13
Quickly building a valuable list of email subscribers

3 READ ME · 43
Effective strategies to get your emails opened and read

4 TALK TO ME · 63
Writing emails that engage and persuade

5 BUY ME · 79
Turning engaged subscribers into paying clients

6 AUTOPILOT MARKETING · 95
Using "autoresponders" to automate your email marketing

7 TAILORING YOUR EMAILS · 103
Using List Segmentation to get the right message to the right subscriber

8 PERSUADING WITH EMAIL · 109
Learning the science of influence

9 MEASURING AND TESTING YOUR EMAIL MARKETING · 119
A simple dashboard to measure the effectiveness of your email marketing

10 EMAIL MARKETING TECHNOLOGY · 127
A guide to tools and technology to support your email marketing

11 YOUR NEXT STEPS · 133

ABOUT THE AUTHOR · 137

INDEX · 139

ACKNOWLEDGMENTS

Many thanks to all my clients and buyers of my email marketing training courses over the years. And special thanks to the smart email marketers you'll see mentioned throughout the book who've kindly shared their best practices and insights that have allowed me to ensure this book contains the very latest thinking and experience of "what's working now" in email marketing.

INTRODUCTION

Email is, without doubt, the most powerful marketing tool available in business today.

Bold claim, I know. But the facts bear it out.

When the Direct Marketing Association studied the effectiveness of various types of marketing[1], Email came out way on top with a return on investment of around 41 to 1. Nearly twice that of any other approach. When data analytics firm Custora published the results of their 4-year study into the online buying patterns of over 72 million customers across 14 different industries[2], they showed that over 40 times as many purchases came from links in emails than from Facebook or Twitter.

And when you think about it, it makes sense. You might chat with friends on Facebook. Or check out the updates from your favourite movie star on Twitter. You might even make some initial connections with business contacts on LinkedIn.

But when it's time to get down to business, the chances are you'll use email.

When I first started my own business back in 2007 my goal was to become known as one of the leading experts on attracting and

---

[1] The Direct Marketing Association, *The Power of Direct Marketing*, October 2011.

[2] Custora, *E-Commerce Customer Acquisition Snapshot*, Q2 2013.

winning clients for consultants and coaches. I focused on my website and blog and managed to get lots of traffic from Google. Later on I started using Twitter and built a six figure following. I became known as an expert on LinkedIn and one of the top bloggers to follow in sales and marketing.

But in truth, growth in my business revenue trailed behind growth in my popularity. I was getting lots of website visitors and lots of name-checks. But not quite so many clients. My writing and my work was getting respect, but I wasn't building a deep enough relationship and enough credibility with my audience to convert them into paying clients.

Then a good friend of mine suggested I try email marketing. I'd avoided it for years. It felt old hat. A bit cheesy if I'm honest. But he twisted my arm and I gave it a try.

Within months I saw an increase in enquiries. And I could trace them directly back to email subscribers. People started replying to my emails and telling me how helpful they'd been or how much they'd resonated with them. My engagement with them went beyond the superficial and intellectual and became personal. Today about 70% of my coaching clients come from the email marketing I do, and over 90% of the people who buy my online products are email subscribers. It's the single most powerful marketing tool I have.

I just wish my friend had twisted my arm earlier.

Why Email Marketing Works

Email marketing is so effective for four simple reasons.

The first is simply that **everyone uses email**.

There are about 3.9 billion email accounts worldwide[3] with around 25% being corporate accounts. And we send 182.9 billion emails *per day*[3] (to put that in perspective, there are roughly 2.7 billion "likes" given on Facebook every day) with 100.5 billion of those emails being business related.

And according to McKinsey[4], we spend two and a half hours a day on business emails if we're employed or run a business. That works out at 50 hours a month.

So while there are plenty of business people who don't use Facebook or Twitter, and most consumers haven't gone near LinkedIn; you can be pretty sure that everyone has an email address, they use it frequently, and when they use it their brain is engaged: they're not just skimming through pictures of cats and inspirational sayings.

In fact, when you look at communication preferences both online and offline, it turns out that across all age groups, email is by far the preferred method for commercial communications. Between 65-78% of adults (depending on age group) name it as their number one preference compared to 0-4% who prefer social media[5].

The second reason email marketing is so effective is that when you do it right, **email is personal**.

When you read material on a website, blog or even on a social media site you know it's a broadcast. You know it's meant for multiple people and you read or watch in that context.

---

[3] Source: Radicati, Email Statistics Report, April 2013.

[4] McKinsey, *The social economy: Unlocking value and productivity through social technologies*, July 2012

[5] Merkle, *The View From The Digital Inbox*, July 2011.

But emails are different. They sit in your inbox next to messages from your friends, relatives, colleagues and clients. There's just something about receiving an email in your own personal inbox that makes it feel like it's been made just for you. Especially if the email is skilfully written in the same style as the emails you get from friends and colleagues.

And typically the rules of play with email are that we try to read whatever comes into our inbox or we at least look at it and scan it. We feel uncomfortable if we miss stuff going through our inbox, just in case it was important. With blogs and social media, not so much.

That means that, provided you've got permission, email marketing is a much more certain route to reaching your ideal clients than to broadcast on the web. You can email regularly and proactively, knowing that while not everyone is going to open and read your emails you stand a decent chance. With social media you're reliant on them being around at the time you send out your message. And increasingly with Facebook, your messages only show up for a small percentage of the people who've liked your page. With email you have much more control.

Perhaps the key reason that email works is that **email marketing is perfect for follow up**.

Let's just forget online marketing for a moment and think about how successful businesses operate in the offline world.

For generations, successful marketers and business developers have known that the key to winning customers – especially for high value products and services – is follow up.

When you first come into contact with a potential client it's pretty unlikely they're ready to buy then and there. It may be that the timing's just not right yet: they're not feeling the pain of their problem enough, or they haven't quite decided on the right strategy to address it.

And often, you'll need to build up considerable credibility and trust before your client will be willing to place the success of a critical part of their business or life in your hands.

So depending on your business it may take four, five, eight, ten or more contact points before your potential client will be ready to buy.

That's why in the face-to-face world, successful business developers follow up relentlessly. Not just to nag and ask whether the client is ready yet. But to add value, build credibility and engender trust.

And it's absolutely the same online.

According to Brian Carroll, author of *Lead Generation For The Complex Sale*[6], "Up to 95% of qualified prospects on your Web site are there to research and are not yet ready to talk with a sales rep, but as many as 70% of them will eventually buy a product from you — or your competitors".

So if you want to build the necessary credibility and trust to turn website visitors into paying clients, you've got to have multiple interactions with them. Sadly, one look at your website statistics will show you that often, 70% or more of your website visitors show up once, but then never return.

And that means that 70% or more of your website visitors are highly unlikely to ever become paying clients.

---

[6] Brian Carroll, *Lead Generation for the Complex Sale: Boost the Quality and Quantity of Leads to Increase Your ROI*, McGraw Hill, 2006.

Email marketing gives you that ability to follow up. When people sign up for your emails you can then proactively communicate with them rather than hoping they remember to come back to your site.

And finally, email marketing is **scalable**.

There's nothing as powerful as personalized follow up. But you can only personally follow up with a limited number of potential clients; eventually you just run out of time.

Email marketing allows you to follow up at scale. To keep in touch with thousands, tens of thousands or even hundreds of thousands of potential customers. And with some of the more advanced strategies we talk about in the book, you can make that follow-up experience really feel quite personal for them. You can email them about the things they've expressed interest in or taken action on.

And because you can track and measure email, you can tell who is opening your emails, who is clicking your links, and who is buying from you. That means you can adapt and improve your approach based on facts. You don't have to rely on what experts tell you *should* work, you can see what *really does work for you.*

That ability to communicate pro-actively, personally and regularly makes email marketing an incredibly powerful tool for building relationships, proving credibility and of course, driving sales.

In fact, if you look at the websites of all the social media gurus you'll see just how powerful email marketing is by the prominence they give it.

Chris Brogan, bestselling author of *Social Media 101*[7] and *Google Plus for Business*[8] says "to me the hottest and sexiest social network right now is your inbox". And he walks the talk, too. Prominent on every page and blog post on chrisbrogan.com is a big subscription form to get what he promises is "the best of what I do": his email newsletter.

"Queen of Facebook", Mari Smith does the same. There's a sign up box for her Social Scoop emails above all the social media buttons on her website. It's the same with Amy Porterfield, Lewis Howes, Melanie Duncan and pretty much every other social media expert. They all focus on capturing email addresses so they can speak to you directly in your inbox. They recognize that when it comes down to business, email really is the world's most powerful marketing tool.

How to Get the Most From This Book

The goal of this book is to help you get results from email marketing. Fast.

To do that, you can use it in one of two ways. You can read it through from start to finish to get a complete grounding in email marketing. Or you can use it as a reference book and dip into the relevant sections as you're working on your own email marketing strategies.

---

[7] Chris Brogan, *Social Media 101: Tactics and Tips to Develop Your Business Online*, John Wiley & Sons, 2010.

[8] Chris Brogan, *Google+ for Business: How Google's Social Network Changes Everything*, Que Publishing, 2012.

My suggestion is that you do both. Read through it quickly, make notes on the areas you think will be the most relevant to you, then get going on implementing those changes to your own email marketing and come back to review when needed.

A lot of the ideas and concepts in the book will make sense when you read them. But you won't *really* learn them until you put them into practice in your own business.

At the end of every chapter you'll find a summary of the main points and a list of suggested actions you can take in your own business to implement effective email marketing. Chapter 11 gives you a short checklist you can use to ensure you have all the key elements of email marketing in hand. And if you're trying to understand how the email marketing best practices covered in the book can be implemented, check out the basic technology guide in chapter 10.

To help you get results faster I've created a companion website for the book with free resources that you can use to get you going fast. Head over to http://www.emailpersuasion.com/bonuses and you can register to get access to extra video training resources, templates and examples you can use, and the latest information on email marketing technologies as they evolve. You can also get access to the Email Persuasion Facebook group where you can ask questions and get feedback on your email marketing from me and the other members of the Email Persuasion Community.

Registration is free for all buyers of this book (make sure to register on the bonus page rather than the normal home page so you get access to all the bonus resources for book buyers only).

Your Next Steps

The most important factor in getting results from this book is that you've got to take action. To help you with that, what I'd like you to do right now is write down the goals you'd like to achieve with your email marketing.

They could be high level goals like getting more clients or growing your sales. Or they could be something very specific you have in mind like doubling your subscriber base.

Whatever it is, write down your main goals for email marketing that you'd like this book to help with. And write down when you'd like to achieve those goals by.

Chances are that after reading the book you'll get new ideas for what you want to achieve with email marketing and you'll get more specific and perhaps more ambitious goals. So come back and revisit your goals as you go through the book. But put something down for now to get you going.

1 WINNING CLIENTS WITH EMAIL: THE FOUNDATIONS

If there's one thing that determines your success at email marketing more than any other it's your ability to understand your target clients. Know exactly what's important to them, what interests them, what their problems are, what their hopes and aspirations are, and you'll know how to email them in ways they'll listen to and take action on.

Building this deep client understanding will tell you:

- What will motivate potential clients to sign up for emails from you.

- Which of your products and services you should promote to them.

- How to promote those products and services. What to emphasize, which benefits to highlight, what else you need to communicate to give them confidence.

- How to communicate with potential clients in language that will resonate with them about issues they care about. So they'll open up your emails, pay attention, feel like you understand them, and feel comfortable taking action.

The simplest and most effective way to build this deep level of understanding is to develop one or more *ideal client personas*.

Creating an Ideal Client Persona

An ideal client persona is an in-depth analysis of the key characteristics, demographics, interests, goals and aspirations, problems and issues of a typical target client for you. Rather than taking an average or summary across all your client types, you dive into details for a small number of the most typical ones. By doing that, you can pull out the specifics that create real insight into what will motivate that type of client to buy from or hire you.

Figure 1 outlines a simple process for creating these ideal client personas. You start by deciding which personas you will

Figure 1: Creating an Ideal Client Persona

develop. You can do this by reviewing your current client base (or if you're just starting out, the clients you'd like to have) and identifying which are the ones you'd like more of. Which ones you have the most experience and expertise in working with, which you most enjoy working with, and which you get the best results for. You then pull out the defining characteristics and common factors that make those clients a great fit for you.

For example, a procurement consultant might realize they do their best work for new purchasing directors who have a background outside procurement and are looking for an experienced mentor. A leadership coach may decide that there are two different types of client they love working with: young managers in their first role with profit and loss responsibility, and experienced senior executives looking for a new challenge.

Of course, you have to sanity check your initial ideas to make sure that the economics are going to work for you. Are there enough of those type of clients? Can they afford to pay for your services? Are they used to paying for this sort of service? Can you reach them with your marketing?

You may well have two or three different types of ideal client you work with, but it's rarely wise for a small business to try to develop and act on more than five personas, it just becomes too confusing. When you first start email marketing, concentrate on one persona only. You can add others later.

Your second step is to gather all the information you have on that type of client. Start by documenting what you already know about them. You'll often be surprised by how much you have already. And it can help to picture a specific individual client in your mind.

You may also have access to market research data that you can incorporate into the analysis. Or you may end up starting your own market research if you feel there are too many gaps in your knowledge. You can survey your clients or potential clients to find out what their big problems and challenges and their goals and aspirations are. Or you can speak to some of them one-to-one to get more in depth information.

Try putting yourself in their shoes by going to where they work or where they live and observing them, with their permission of course. Or try actually doing what they do. Sometimes you can see the day-to-day problems they don't notice themselves. Problems that are so ingrained in their normal day-to-day business that they've come to see them as normal operations, not realising the impact they're having.

One of the founding fathers of online marketing, Ken McCarthy calls this the "road repair method of market research":

"Get out of your ivory tower, forget about your world changing ideas, and walk (don't drive) the roadway (i.e. immerse yourself in the customer experience.)

If you do this, you'll invariably find holes and bumps in what's currently being offered profitably in the marketplace. They'll jump right out at you. No high IQ or advanced market research tools required."

Once you've gathered all the information you can, you then start analysing the information to extract insights that you can use in your marketing. I call this process *Customer Insight Mapping*[9].

Customer Insight Mapping is simply a process for drawing out and organising the information you have about your clients into a form that allows you to extract actionable insights. Knowledge that you can do something about in your marketing. It starts with the obvious surface level observations and then goes deeper into the factors that will drive their behaviour.

So let's get going.

First of all, take a large sheet of paper and divide it into diagonal quadrants and label them as in Figure 2.

In the centre, rather than the picture of cogs whirring inside someone's brain, draw or stick a picture of a real person. Strange though it sounds, having an actual picture of your ideal client persona helps make the whole process more real for you, and will help you produce a more detailed and useful persona.

---

[9] Inspired by Empathy Mapping from Alexander Osterwalder and Yves Pigneur, *Business Model Generation*, John Wiley & Sons, August 2010.

Figure 2: Customer Insight Mapping

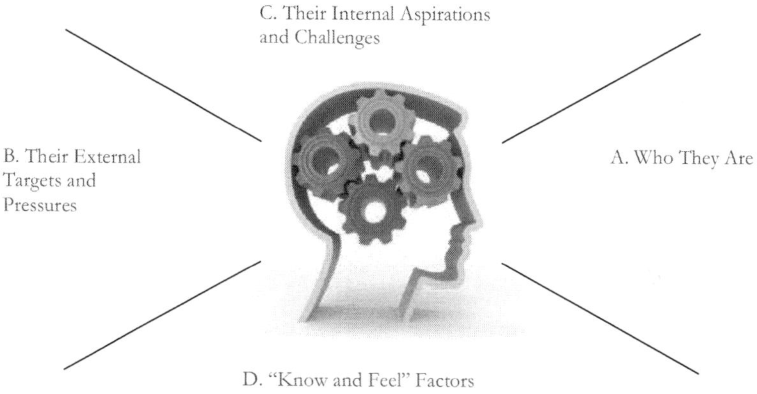

C. Their Internal Aspirations and Challenges

B. Their External Targets and Pressures

A. Who They Are

D. "Know and Feel" Factors

In quadrant A on the right hand side of the page you're going to summarize all the basic facts and figures and demographics you know about this ideal client. How old they are, what sex they typically are. Married or single, kids or no kids. Their level of education. Their typical work experience and career path that got them where they are today. Their current role. What their interests are outside of work. Who they admire. Who they hate.

Of course, you won't know all of this. And some of it may be very variable even within your ideal client group. But write down what you can.

Next, move across to quadrant B on the left of the page. Here you'll write down what you know about the typical external targets and pressures placed upon them.

If they run a business, what are the profitability and growth goals – perhaps set by the shareholders? What moves are their competitors making? How are their customers changing? What about new legislation, environmental issues, changes in their supplier base? If they're in an employed role, what targets have they been set by their boss?

This is where the insights begin to appear. Most businesses know what their customers have told them they need. But when they understand the targets they've been set, the pressures they're under, what their customers' customers want from them, they're often able to identify unspoken needs that can be even more powerful motivators.

Next, move up to quadrant C at the top of the page and start writing down everything you know about your client's internal goals and aspirations and the big personal challenges and problems they face day to day.

So as a business owner, they may have an official target of growing sales by 20% this year. But personally, they may want to double the sales over the next three years so they can sell the business and retire. The head of accounts receivable may have been set goals of reducing write-offs by 20%, but their personal aspiration may be to get a promotion and move more into general finance. Their personal goals are often much bigger motivators for them than the targets they've been set.

With these personal goals and aspirations, the key to really understanding them is to ask "why?" until you reach something emotional. Your ideal client may typically want to earn a six figure sum, but why is that? Perhaps it's to allow them to focus on work they can enjoy. Or maybe it's so they can pay off the mortgage and provide for their family without any worries about peaks and troughs in income. Knowing what these underlying reasons are allows you to touch on them in your emails which become much more powerful as a result.

You should also try to capture their day-to-day problems and annoyances. What stands in their way? What do they grumble about? Those may not be things they'd pay a fortune to address, but if what you offer helps with them it'll add to your appeal. And they'll always be interested in hearing useful information that helps them deal with those problems.

The final stage is to move down to quadrant D at the bottom. This is where you extract and extrapolate from the other quadrants to identify what your ideal clients would need to know and feel to be comfortable hiring you or buying from you.

So out of all the targets, goals and problems you've identified so far, which are the ones that match with what you can deliver, and are big enough issues for them to care about? What are the big pains you relieve them of? What are the big gains you help them achieve? What are the impacts of those problems on them and their business? What would the results look and feel like if they achieved their goals?

And what would they need to see from you to believe that you were the right person to work with or buy from?

So for example, do they need to know you've worked with people just like them and achieved great results? Or are they more likely to want to know you've trodden in their footsteps and done what they want to achieve yourself? Do they care about how they would get on with you personally? Or that you believe in the same causes as them? What are they frightened of? What risks do they see in working with you? Are they worried about looking foolish or weak to the rest of the organization? Are they worried about making a big investment that isn't going to pay off and that's going to damage their position in the hierarchy?

These more intangible factors are the things you need to get across to them in your interactions with them (i.e. your emails) before they'll be ready to buy.

Now, of course, this process isn't easy. As you work your way through it you'll find yourself racking your brain struggling to answer some of the questions. Or you may find that there's not a single answer, that there are a lot of options. No matter. Just get down what you can. It will all work to raise your understanding of your clients and you can continue to refine and improve your ideal client personas over time as you get to know them better.

Let's look a simplified example to show you how this might work out in practice.

Our hero is Mike, an experienced procurement consultant and ex Chief Procurement Officer of a large corporate. He's identified his ideal client as Tony Jones, a newly promoted procurement director. Someone who probably worked in a management role in manufacturing or supply chain before being given the procurement role. Here's an abbreviated version of his Customer Insight Map.

Figure 3: Example Customer Insight Map

C. Internal Aspirations and Challenges
- Wants to make a big impact: 20%+ savings.
- Goal is promotion to senior role in manufacturing.
- New to procurement. Doesn't feel in control. Not sure what "levers to pull" to get results.

B. External Targets and Pressures
- 10% year-on-year external cost reduction.
- No increase in procurement headcount.
- "Get procurement under control".

Tony Jones

A. Who They Are
- Mid 30s, male, 1 young child.
- University educated.
- Previous role as mid level manager in manufacturing.
- Works long hours, looks up to results oriented executives.

D. "Know and Feel" Factors
- Big personal win is to get 20%+ savings.
- Wants to know he will get credit for improvements rather than consultants taking the glory.
- Needs someone he can trust: sounding board, someone experienced to call the bluff of the procurement team.

What Mike has identified is that Tony has ambitious goals and wants to use this role as a stepping stone into general management, but his lack of procurement experience leaves him feeling exposed and unable to directly influence the results of his department. That means that Tony will be more open to approaches that help him gain understanding and control over procurement rather than just a "black box" approach to making improvements. And he'll identify with stories and examples of procurement leaders who went on to other more senior roles.

And, of course, Tony is typical of very many potential clients Mike has. That's why he picked this persona to flesh out.

This is just an simplified example but I hope you can see how the process of working through these factors step-by-step allows you to build up a picture of what your ideal client would be interested in hearing about in your emails, and the additional messages you need to get across to them for them to be ready to hire you or buy from you.

We'll be returning to the outputs from the Customer Insight Map time and time again as we look at what will motivate your potential clients to subscribe to your emails and what to write in each email you send. Their goals and aspiration, challenges and issues will be the topics that you're going to write about because those are the things that they're interested in and care about. They're the things related to their big important goals in their life or the problems that they have.

By using those as the foundation of what you write, you can guarantee that when you're sending emails your potential clients will be interested in them. You don't start from what you have and what you want to tell them about, *you start from what you know they're already interested in.*

Many years ago legendary copywriter, Robert Collier, said that you have to "start by entering the conversation already going on in your prospect's mind". And that's exactly what you're doing here by focusing the topics of your emails on the things that your ideal clients are already thinking about: the problems they suffer from and the aspirations they have. That ensures that your emails are the sort that they'll want to open.

You'll then weave the "know and feel" factors into your emails by using them to illustrate the topics you're emailing about.

So if Mike knows that Tony is interested in decreasing external spend by 20%, but needs to convince him that he has many years of experience in procurement before he'll hire him, then instead of just writing an email with "7 tips for cutting external spend", he can illustrate that email with examples from his own personal experience. He can tell the story of how over many years as a procurement director he learnt seven important strategies that he used time and time again to decrease external costs.

Tony will open up the email and read it because of the advice on cutting costs. But in the process, he'll become aware of Mike's years of experience, which will begin to position him as the person he'll want to call when he's ready to buy.

The Power of Personas

Many people understand the concept of personas intellectually, but worry that it won't work for them. They fear that their client base is just too diverse and that any persona they develop won't be "close enough" to their different clients.

So instead they write very general emails, trying to appeal to as many people as possible. And unfortunately, general emails tend to wash over people: they have no impact.

And the truth is that a persona doesn't have to perfect to be effective.

The best way to imagine personas is like an archery target. The persona you draw up is at the centre, the bull's-eye. Not all your potential clients are in that same place. They share some things in common with the persona you draw up (at minimum they'd all benefit from your products or services), but they're scattered around the target in the inner and outer circles rather than all being at the centre.

When you write emails specifically for your ideal client persona you're firing an arrow at the bull's-eye. If you hit, then not only will your message resonate perfectly with people who match that ideal client persona, but you'll be pretty close to all the other clients on the target. Certainly much closer than if you just shoot an arrow randomly into the air by writing a generic email.

Having that ideal client persona in mind makes your emails more specific and "real". So they click with potential clients even if they're that bit different to the persona you write them for.

Summary

Developing a detailed client persona and building deep understanding of your ideal clients is the critical foundation for all effective email marketing. Investing the time to understand those clients' goals and aspirations, problems and challenges and what they need to know and feel to be ready to hire you will enable you to write emails that they're motivated to open, read and take action on.

Your Next Steps

- Select a client type to profile based on who you work the best with, get the best results for, and that's the most economically viable for you.

- Gather all the knowledge and research you have on that type of client and create a Customer Insight Map.

- Identify the big problems, challenges, goals and aspirations that your ideal client cares about. And figure out what they need to know and feel about you to be ready to hire you.

- Summarize those big factors – you'll be using them to shape what you offer to get subscribers and what you focus your emails on.

2 SIGN ME UP: HOW TO QUICKLY BUILD A VALUABLE SUBSCRIBER LIST

Before you can start emailing, persuading, engaging or relationship building, you need a "list" of people to email to. And for many businesses, this is a big stumbling block.

It's perfectly possible to run a highly profitable business with an email list with just a few thousand names and email addresses on it, sometimes even just a few hundred. But for many people, their biggest problem is that they only have a handful of people who've signed up to their emails. So this chapter will show you how to quickly build up a database of enthusiastic subscribers.

Should You Buy an Email List?

When you're just starting off with email marketing it can be very tempting to try to short cut the process by buying a list of names that somebody else has collected that you can then email, but there are a number of downsides to that.

The first reason is that any lists you buy are rarely targeted on your ideal clients. They may be segmented by job title or geography or business size or sector, but what you can't do is buy a list of people interested in what you have to offer.

The second reason is that whoever you buy your email list from, you never really know exactly how they've collected those names. You've probably experienced yourself getting a phone call from someone "just confirming your name and email address" and claiming you're already on their directory. Very often that's how your name gets onto these email lists.

Or you've bought something from a website and at the bottom of the order page there's a tiny little check box that you forget to uncheck or you struggle to work out whether you should check it or uncheck it if you don't want to receive marketing emails.

Or it could be that as a condition of joining your Chamber of Commerce or other membership organisation you go into their directory, which is then sold on to businesses or given to other members.

In this case you joined the Chamber of Commerce because you wanted to go to events and meet other chamber members, not receive marketing emails. It was just a condition of entry that you went onto the list.

Few people are on any of those commercial lists for reasons that would make them enthusiastic to receive emails from someone they've never heard of before.

So the chances are if you buy one of those lists and you then start emailing people, you're not going to get a very good reaction. You may get spam complaints; you'll probably get very low open rates and click through rates because the people on it weren't expecting emails from you about the topics that you're going to email them about.

And if you're using any of the most common email marketing services, almost all of them prohibit you from uploading bought email lists for the very reason that they tend to get lots of spam complaints and they want to protect their reputation. By uploading a bought email list you'll very likely be breaking the terms and conditions of your email service provider.

Generally speaking, buying an email list rarely produces good results. If you do decide that it's your only way to get going fast, then rather than just starting to send your regular emails to the people on the list, send them an offer to sign up for a free report or other high value giveaway. Only a small percentage will do so, but you've now identified the people who are actually interested in the topics you email about and who will value hearing from you regularly.

Adding People to Your Email List Without Permission

I'm sure this has happened to you before: you meet someone at an event. You chat for a while and exchange business cards. Then a few days later you get their email newsletter. Or you were in the audience when they did a presentation and again, you somehow end up on their mailing list.

They didn't mention it. You didn't agree to subscribe, but for some reason they think it's a good idea to start sending you regular emails.

Just like buying a list, this rarely produces positive results. If you just happen to meet someone at an event, they may have given you a business card but they haven't given you permission to email them regularly via your newsletter. They're expecting that maybe you'll call them or email them personally as a one off. But they're certainly not expecting to appear on your newsletter list and get it every week or every month.

Similarly if someone is in the audience for a presentation of yours and they gave their email address to the organizer when they signed up then again, they weren't expecting to get regular emails from you.

In the worst case, what will happen is your emails will get marked as spam and that will damage your reputation and you may get your personal email servers closed down or barred by your email marketing service provider. At best all that's going to happen is they'll ignore you or maybe even just build up a simmering resentment.

Certainly whenever I get added to the email newsletters of people I meet then even if they're really nice people, even if I got on well with them, if they put me on their email list without permission I get annoyed. Any further emails they send just annoy me even more.

Emailing without permission like this actually damages your relationships. It shows you don't really think or care about them. You just see them as yet another name to add to a list and maybe try to sell something to.

Now there are ways in which you can get people who you've met onto your email list. The simplest and most direct is to suggest it to them while you're face to face by saying something along the lines of "By the way I've got a free report that I give away along with regular emails with tips on X, Y and Z. Would you like me to hook you up with a copy?" Or email them after you've met with a one off personal email and offer the same thing, but don't sign them up until they agree.

For existing contacts you can go through the same process to build an initial email list. Compile a hit list of potential subscribers from contacts you have on email, in your CRM system, or from that pile of business cards in a shoebox. Then contact them as above to offer them your incentive and regular emails. Not all of them will sign up. In fact most won't unless your incentive is very strong. But it will give you a clean database to start from.

With your current and recent customers you can add them to a different list for sending customer service and follow-up emails rather than emails aimed at getting them to buy. In this case there's usually no need to ask permission as you have an existing business relationship and as a customer they'd expect you to keep in touch.

The Right Way to Get Email Subscribers

The right way to get email subscribers is to *ask permission*. To make them an offer to receive your emails (probably linked to some free gift for subscribing) and to sign them up if they agree.

As we've already described, you can do that face to face. You can make the offer at the end of a presentation, in direct mail, over the telephone or even in a print ad.

But most of the time you'll make that offer on your website and that's what we'll focus on here. The exact same principles apply, however, wherever you make your offer.

Technically speaking you'll present website visitors with the option to subscribe (or "opt-in") by showing them a form (usually known as an "opt-in form") where they can enter their email address and often their name and submit that form to agree to receive your emails.

How many subscribers you get and who they are is determined by where you show that form, how often, what it looks like, how you describe your emails, what you give away as an incentive to subscribe, how you mitigate any concerns they might have and any further proof you give that subscribing would be a good thing for them.

We'll cover each of those factors and how to get more of the right sort of people subscribing in this chapter.

A Word About Traffic

The focus of this book is email marketing, not getting traffic to your website – that's a huge topic in its own right. But for those of you wanting some quick tips on getting more traffic to your site to get more subscribers, here's what I've found works for me.

The key in my experience is to focus on the *quality* of visitors to your site – not just the *quantity*.

I've found the very best website visitors, the ones most likely to sign up for my emails, are visitors coming based on a recommendation. So if someone else recommends me and gives a link to one of my landing pages from their site or in an email to their subscribers, or if they endorse me by running a joint webinar with me, then those visitors are highly likely to sign up.

Next best is search engine traffic – either paid or organic search. Here, your visitors are searching for specific information that your site provides – so they're likely to sign up to get it.

Social media visitors tend to be more interested in getting a quick fix of free information. A certain percentage will subscribe, but fewer than other sources.

So my personal focus for traffic is partnering with others to get endorsed traffic (which also helps my search engine optimisation by giving me links from sites in my field). I'll do that by offering to write guest articles for other high profile websites in my field with a link back to my email opt-in page. Or I'll do an interview for them. Or run a joint webinar where I present some of my best material to their audience and they promote the webinar (including opting in to my list) via their own email marketing.

The "Opt-in Formula"

There are four big factors that determine whether someone who sees one of your opt-in forms is going to complete it and subscribe or ignore it and click away. These factors are summarised in the Opt-in Formula.

$$\text{Opt In Rate} = \frac{V + I}{F + R}$$

V stands for (long term) Value. That's the perceived value that a potential subscriber will see in getting your emails week in, week out, day in, day out, or however frequently you send them.

I is a (short-term) Incentive that you give to them in order to encourage them to subscribe. So it could be a free report you give away, a CD, a video etc. Something you offer them for free that's in a related area to what you're going to be emailing about.

F stands for Friction, the things that will slow down someone and get in the way of them signing up. So if your forms have too many fields or they can't find them on the page or the button doesn't stand out; all that creates friction, slows people down and discourages them from signing up.

Finally, **R stands for (perceived) Risk**. So if they feel as if they're taking a risk by giving you their email address, that they might get a bunch of spam from you or they might be signed up for some dreadful scheme, then they'll be more reticent to sign up.

Let's look at each of the factors in turn to see how to increase or decrease it as appropriate.

Long Term Value

Whenever you give website visitors the chance to get regular emails from you, they're going to make an assessment (probably subconsciously) of whether they're going to get value from those emails.

Now if you're already a pretty well-known name in your field. If you've written a couple of successful books, if you often present at conferences, or you're just known for being insightful in your subject then this initial perception is going to be pretty positive. Often it won't take much more to get people to subscribe.

For most of us however, we have to do a little more.

One thing we can do is to have a lot of great free content on our website. If potential subscribers have read our articles, listened to our audios or watched our videos and been impressed, then the chances are that they'll assume they'll get more of the same from our regular emails and be encouraged to subscribe.

We can also increase the perceived long term value by the way we describe our emails. Nowadays many businesses mention a newsletter on their website, but the phrase 'newsletter' doesn't have any implied value in it. In fact the word 'news' is probably something you don't want to hear from a potential supplier. Who cares whether Mary in accounts has had a birthday? What you would like to get is useful, valuable information.

So instead of calling it an email newsletter, I call mine 'client winning tips via email'. Or you could call it a 'divorce survival bulletin'. Or 'the cash flow accelerator emails' or 'tax cutting tips'.

Each of these names implies some kind of value or outcome your potential subscribers will get from your emails. To come up with a good name, go back to your customer insight map for your ideal clients and look at the big problems, challenges, goals and aspirations your clients have. If you can name your emails to relate to those big goals and problems then they're likely to see they'll get value by subscribing to them.

Short Term Incentive

As well as the value inherent in your emails themselves, potential subscribers will be motivated to subscribe if you offer them some kind of incentive.

There's a balance to be drawn here. If they're only subscribing for the incentive then the chances are that they'll tune out of your emails pretty quickly. You'd probably get a lot of subscribers by offering them $100 to join up. But what you'd end up doing is building an email list of people who wanted the cash, rather than people interested in how you can help them.

So you have to make sure that your incentive is related to what it is you're going to be emailing them about and the kind of products and services you sell.

The most common form of incentive to offer is a free report or video or audio download which offers ideas and solutions to a pressing problem your ideal clients have. This is often called a **Lead Magnet** – as it attracts qualified leads.

Other forms of lead magnet could be a quiz or self-assessment that people complete and sign up to get their answers. Or a short training course delivered periodically via email, a template or spread sheet, a resource guide, or even a piece of software.

One current trend is to offer "free registration" to get access to resources rather than "subscribing" to emails. This is taking advantage of the fact that most web users are used to registering for services they find valuable. The more your opt-in process looks like something they've done a dozen times before, like signing up for Facebook or Twitter or for a free account with an online app or webmail service, then the more natural it will seem to do so with you too.

Using this type of registration approach you'd put your lead magnet and other free resources into a private membership site that subscribers get access to by signing up. This feeling of exclusive access and similarity with other online services may well result in increased sign up rates. Right now it's too early to tell, but a number of big online marketers like Copyblogger are going down this route.

Your goal with a lead magnet is more than just to attract subscribers. You also want to begin your relationship with them as effectively as possible by establishing your credibility and creating a sense of reciprocation by giving them something that will help solve an important problem for them.

And a lead magnet also works to qualify subscribers because by signing up for it, they've shown they want a solution to a problem that you have bigger service or product based solutions for.

Creating an Attractive Lead Magnet

The most important factor in whether a lead magnet is attractive to your ideal clients is the topic it covers. Or more accurately, the results they'll get from it. So irrespective of whether it's a free report, a video, an audio, the key is that it needs to address a big important and urgent problem that many of your clients have.

There are a number of different ways you can identify good topics for a lead magnet. Start by reviewing your customer insight map for your ideal client, then:

- List the last 10 client problems you've worked on or questions you've been asked by clients recently

- Think of one painful thing all your clients seem to run into

- Think of the "first speed bump" your clients face on their journey to achieve their goals

- Think of an overarching framework or concept or root cause for the big issues your clients face

Jason Leister, who does coaching and consulting for copywriters and online entrepreneurs, has a lead magnet, which is a short report on how to answer the question "How much do you charge?" Because that's a question that every copywriter or independent professional gets asked at some point and often they don't have a great answer.

The "first speed bump" approach focuses on the initial problems your clients face. If you help them with leadership, then building their own confidence is often a first step before working with them on bigger issues like teambuilding, motivation and setting a vision. A business coach might choose to focus their lead magnet on ways of improving cash flow: a necessary first step for many businesses before addressing any longer term issues like growing revenue or building staff capabilities.

The first speed bump is often a good topic for a lead magnet because many potential clients get stuck at that first hurdle. By helping them get quick results with that initial problem, you'll give them the confidence to work with you on bigger issues.

Once you've got your topic for a lead magnet you then have to make sure that people can see that the topic is going to be valuable to them. It needs to be clear from the name and the description of the lead magnet that they'll get immediate value.

If it looks like they'll have to spend weeks learning about the topic or read a War and Peace-like tome just to get going then they're going to head off and find something quicker and easier. The faster potential subscribers see that they'll get value; the more likely they are to subscribe.

Here's a good example of how to position a lead magnet from web designer and marketer D Bnonn Tennant:

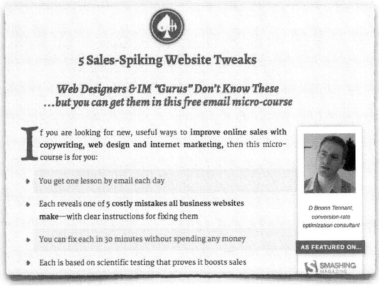

5 Sales-Spiking Website Tweaks

Web Designers & IM "Gurus" Don't Know These ...but you can get them in this free email micro-course

If you are looking for new, useful ways to **improve online sales with copywriting, web design and internet marketing**, then this micro-course is for you:

- You get one lesson by email each day

- Each reveals one of **5 costly mistakes all business websites make**—with clear instructions for fixing them

- You can fix each in 30 minutes without spending any money

- Each is based on scientific testing that proves it boosts sales

D Bnonn Tennant, conversion-rate optimization consultant

AS FEATURED ON...

SMASHING MAGAZINE

Figure 4: Bnonn Tennant's lead magnet

Notice how Bnonn gets straight to the bottom line. He doesn't talk about improving your website, he talks about "sales spiking website tweaks". And by using the word "tweaks" he's implying that they're not major changes that will take ages to implement. You'll get results fast.

Entrepreneur and advisor to micro businesses Danny Iny gives away a video training course that shows you how to "get more cash out of any business, website or blog in under 30 days, without spending money, working more hours or hiring staff!" It's a bold claim, but an attractive one.

In both cases you can tell quite easily from the offer they're making and the language they're using exactly whom they'd like as a client. In one case it's someone who wants to get more sales, but specifically from their website. In the other it's someone more focused on the profitability and cash flow of their entire business. That's because both Danny and Bnonn have developed clear personas for their ideal clients and have focused their lead magnets on what's important to those people and used the sort of language that will resonate with them.

Here's another example, a lead magnet for a boat club:

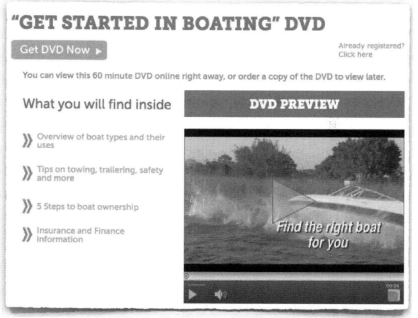

Figure 5: The "Get Started In Boating" lead magnet

It's a free DVD called 'Get Started In Boating'. So they're targeting people just getting into boating. It doesn't show you how to sail your boat brilliantly or sell it, or maintain it. It focuses on the initial speed bump problems of how do I buy a boat? What types of boat are there to buy? How do I get it insured and financed? How do I tow and trailer it? So they're focusing very much on the first problems that someone will have when they're just getting into boating, which makes them an ideal client for a boat club.

Each of these lead magnets focuses on giving immediate value that's specifically tailored to what their ideal clients are looking for. The lead magnet doesn't have to be particularly big, or in any particularly fancy format. Video and software have higher perceived value than just an audio or a PDF, but the biggest factor is the value contained in the lead magnet. If I knew the winning lottery numbers for next week, for example, you wouldn't much worry about whether I got those numbers to you in a video, an audio, or just scribbled on a scruffy piece of paper. And it's the same with lead magnets. It's the value of the content that counts.

If you're writing a report that helps your potential clients to solve an important problem then something like five to ten pages of text with a few diagrams is easily enough. Or 15-30 minutes of video or audio. It doesn't have to be very large.

In fact creating a very large lead magnet, although it might convey credibility and expertise, also has a significant downside.

People are going to download it or get a copy of it, they're going to see that it's 40 pages long, or it's a two-hour video and they're going to put it to one side and think, "Oh I'll look at that later."

And then they'll probably never come back to it. Other priorities will always get in the way. And because they haven't managed to read or watch your free lead magnet, the chances are they'll be reluctant to buy one of your paid products or to phone you to work with them because in the back of their mind they'll always be thinking, "I haven't even managed to get through his free report, there's no point in buying anything from him yet."

If you're not a natural writer and you're struggling to create a report, then a shortcut to producing a valuable lead magnet quickly is what I call the **expert interview**.

All of us, if we know what we're talking about, could answer four or five questions in our field that our clients typically ask us. In fact we probably do that most days as our customers, clients and prospects email or phone us with questions.

To create an expert interview lead magnet all you do is write down four or five good questions in your field that you can answer that will provide useful information to your potential clients. Then get a friend to ask you the questions in the form of an interview and record them. You can use an audio recorder if you're meeting face to face, or get them to call you on Skype or use a free teleconference service and record the call.

You can then turn that interview into an audio download or you can put it onto a CD for a couple of dollars, or even get a transcript for a few dollars more. That interview will then be perceived as pretty high value. It doesn't have to be word perfect because when experts are interviewed normally on TV or radio they're not word perfect. And that interview format creates a perception of you as being an expert because the people who get interviewed tend to be experts.

If you follow that process you can get something that will be perceived as high value by your potential clients and you can have it up and running in less than an hour.

Decreasing Friction

Friction is the set of things on your site that will slow down and hamper potential subscribers. This often takes the form of distractions. So if someone is thinking about completing your opt-in form, but suddenly an image on your site changes, it'll draw their eye away. Or they might spot an interesting blog post and head off to read it.

So the first step to reducing friction is to remove distractions from near your opt-in forms. The easiest way to do this is to use dedicated landing pages wherever you can. Whenever you can direct traffic to your website, send it to a specific page focused on offering your lead magnet and getting an opt-in instead of having that traffic just go to your generic homepage.

If you're using pay-per-click advertising for example, or if you do guest blog posts and you have a link in the author bio or in the links from your social media profiles, don't send visitors to your homepage where maybe the opt-in rate is 2-4% if you're lucky. Send them to a dedicated landing page that offers them your lead magnet and the opt-in rate is 10% or more because that's the only thing that that page does.

Figure 6 (on the next page) is an example of one of the simple landing pages on my site that visitors go to if they click on a link from one of my social media profiles or if I've written a guest blog post for someone else's site. All it has is a picture of the lead magnet, a description, and the opt-in form. It's clear what you can get from opting in and there's nothing else to distract you.

Directing visitors from pay-per-click advertising to your home page is one of the most basic errors and wastes of money in online marketing. Yet I still see it being done time and time again by even very large companies. With pay-per-click, particularly if your adverts are triggered by specific searches on Google or Bing, you have the opportunity to send people to a specific web page directly related to what they searched for. Don't waste that click by sending them to your home page, the most generic page on your site.

Figure 6: A simple landing page from ianbrodie.com

Similarly, whenever you write a guest blog post, don't do what most people do and at the end of the article just say "for more great resources head over to mysite.com". Send them to a specific landing page where you offer them a lead magnet that directly relates to and builds on the article.

You can either say something like "Ian Brodie is the author of the free report, 5 Simple Marketing Tweaks That Will Get You More Clients" and link to a landing page with that report as a lead magnet. Or even better, you can give a logical reason for getting the report: "To learn the fastest ways of putting the tips from this article into practice and start getting results, download Ian's free report, 5 Simple Marketing Tweaks That Will Get You More Clients". By tying together the article they've just read with your lead magnet you make it more likely that readers will click through to get it.

Make sure you have a strong headline on your landing page too that clearly express what they'll get from your lead magnet and regular emails. Here's an example from Facebook guru Brian Moran:

Figure 7: Brian Moran's Timeline Blueprint Landing Page

You can see immediately what you'll get from the lead magnet: a Facebook landing page template that increased sales by 53.1%.

Even simple changes to headlines can make a big difference to opt-in rates. In a case study reported by whichtestwon.com, Reebok made a simple change to the headline of their opt-in form from "Join the Reebok Newsletter" to "Join and Save". That addition of a benefit (savings) to the headline increased their opt-in rate by 40%.

So if you can direct traffic to a specific landing page where you can focus on getting the opt-in and removing all the distractions and having a very strong headline that describes the value that people will get by opting in then you should do so.

Sometimes, however, you won't be able to do this. Traffic from social media sites, for example, usually comes to specific blog posts or other pieces of content on your site. As often does organic search traffic.

In these cases, your job is to give your visitors what they came for (the article or other resource) but to also give them as many opportunities to see the value of opting in as possible.

Figure 8: An opt-in form on the sidebar of smartpassiveincome.com

The minimum is to have an opt-in form in the sidebar of your site. You've probably seen this on very many sites. And that's the problem: familiarity breeds blindness on the web. If every site has an opt-in form in the exact same place on their sidebar, most people begin to ignore it.

So typically you'll also need to put opt-in forms on other places on your site to get the attention of visitors.

Rising Internet star Marie Forleo's home page is dominated by a huge header encouraging you to opt-in.

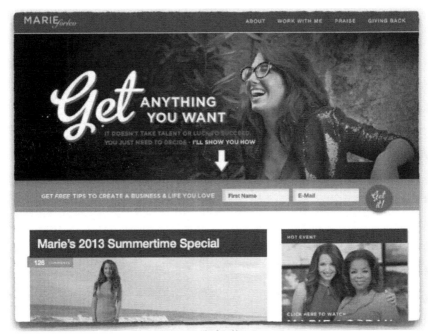

Figure 9: An opt-in form in the page header at marieforleo.com

It has a strong headline, and it's kind of unmissable.

Other sites put opt-in forms in places where they'll be seen if you've already taken an interest in what they have to say. That way they're not interrupting people who aren't ready yet, but they capture the attention of people who are.

Peep Laja's ConversionXL site, for example, includes an opt-in form at the end of every blog post (with the logic being that if you're interested enough to read to the end of an article you may well be interested enough to subscribe for more).

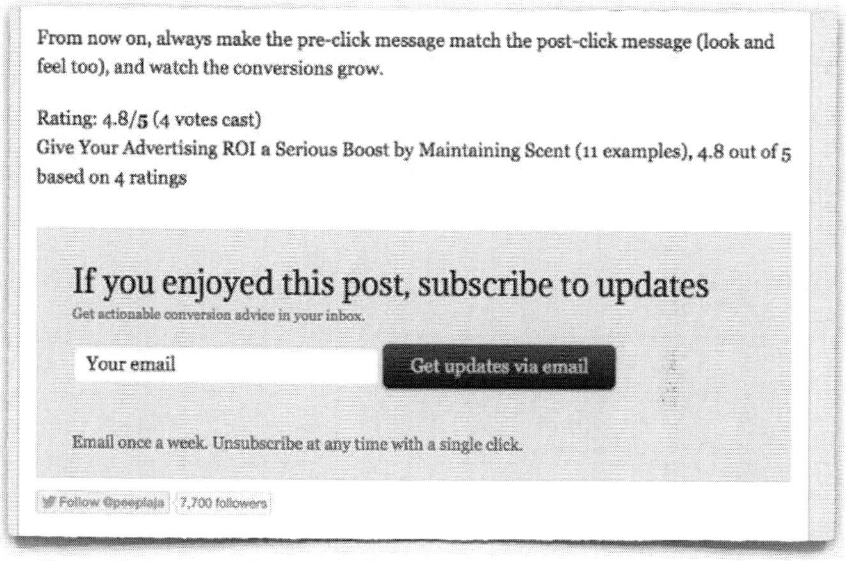

From now on, always make the pre-click message match the post-click message (look and feel too), and watch the conversions grow.

Rating: 4.8/5 (4 votes cast)
Give Your Advertising ROI a Serious Boost by Maintaining Scent (11 examples), 4.8 out of 5 based on 4 ratings

If you enjoyed this post, subscribe to updates

Get actionable conversion advice in your inbox.

Your email   Get updates via email

Email once a week. Unsubscribe at any time with a single click.

Follow @peeplaja | 7,700 followers

Figure 10: An opt-in form at the bottom of a blog post on conversionxl.com

Another example of placing an opt-in form where only people who've indicated a prior interest will see is your "About" page. If someone's made the effort to click on your About page then they've indicated they want to find out more about you. So why not give them the opportunity to subscribe to your regular emails by putting an opt-in form on the page?

Derek Halpern does this very effectively at socialtriggers.com. Rather than making his About page all about him, he first talks about what visitors will get from the site. Which leads nicely in to saying that the way to get the most from the site and him is to subscribe to his emails. He then has an opt-in form after each section on the page, giving visitors both a good reason and multiple opportunities to opt in.

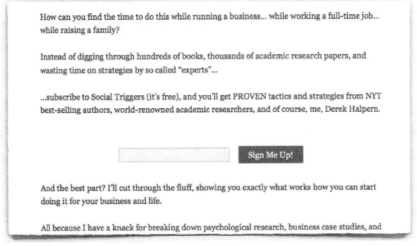

How can you find the time to do this while running a business... while working a full-time job... while raising a family?

Instead of digging through hundreds of books, thousands of academic research papers, and wasting time on strategies by so called "experts"...

...subscribe to Social Triggers (it's free), and you'll get PROVEN tactics and strategies from NYT best-selling authors, world-renowned academic researchers, and of course, me, Derek Halpern.

Sign Me Up!

And the best part? I'll cut through the fluff, showing you exactly what works how you can start doing it for your business and life.

All because I have a knack for breaking down psychological research, business case studies, and

Figure 11: An opt-in form on the About page at socialtriggers.com

In each of these cases what you've got is one prominent form, either at the top of the side bar or running across the top of the site, that people see wherever they go. After that the only time they see a form is when they take action. So they've clicked on the About page and they see a form there. Or they've scrolled to the bottom of an article and they've seen a form there.

Because you're only showing them forms when they're taking an action and expressing interest then it doesn't become too intrusive. It doesn't destroy their experience exploring your site.

To Pop or Not to Pop?

One of the most controversial areas when it comes to opt-in forms is the use of "popups": forms which appear when you're browsing a site and typically stop you seeing the site until you either opt-in or click close.

Popups have been used for many years on the web and have traditionally been associated with the seedier end of internet marketing. They were typically ugly and kept interrupting what you were trying to do.

Nowadays, popups are much better looking and can be controlled so that they don't interrupt the browsing experience of repeat visitors or existing subscribers, or of people who've only just come to a website.

Figure 12: A professional looking popup from marieforleo.com

The reason pop ups have persisted is that they work. There are numerous case studies on the web showing increased opt-in rates of 200%, 500% or more from installing a pop up.

You could argue that maybe those extra subscribers aren't as high quality because they just filled in the form to get rid of the popup, and that may indeed be true – though no one has really collected much data on this.

Right now, what we know is:

- Using a popup *will* increase your opt-in rate.

- But it will also annoy a lot of your website visitors, including current subscribers and clients. And it may not create the kind of impression you're hoping new visitors get of you.

If you do decide to use a popup, make sure that the popup

looks professional, and try to avoid it appearing for visitors who've already opted in.

As a less intrusive alternative to a popup, some sites (mine included) use a "welcome gate". With a welcome gate, the very first time a visitor comes to your home page they're redirected to a dedicated landing page that offers your lead magnet. It's optional: there's a link just to go through to the normal home page. But it's almost as effective as a popup in terms of opt-in rate.

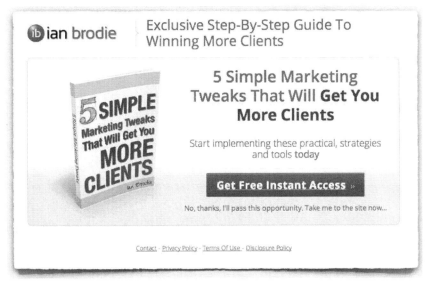

Figure 13: The "Welcome Gate" shown to first time visitors to ianbrodie.com

And because you're only showing the page to visitors who chose to go to your home page rather than those who came looking for specific blog posts or other resources, you're usually not getting in the way of them accessing the information they came for. And once they've seen the welcome gate once, it's not shown to them again. My own testing has shown that a welcome gate will get around a 10% opt-in rate compared to the 2-3% you'd get on a typical blog post.

Keep It Simple for Subscribers

One final element that can reduce friction is to decrease the amount of information you collect on your opt-in forms.

Some businesses try to collect as much information as possible, asking for subscriber's full names, their business name, job title and even telephone number. But the more information you ask potential subscribers to type in, the more difficult and arduous it will seem to them. When they make the mental balance between the value they'll get from subscribing and the pain they have to go through to do so, they may well end up deciding not to bother.

That's particularly true if you're collecting sensitive information. Ask for someone's phone number and they'll assume you're going to call to try to sell them something. Ask for their job title or the size of their business and they'll assume you're doing some sort of qualification to decide if they're worth selling to. In either case many people will either put in fake information or not bother subscribing at all.

In fact, many marketers have gone as far as removing all fields from their forms other than the email address, and have reported that their opt-in rates have increased[10].

There's no definitive answer here: Hubspot found that the number of fields made very little difference to subscription rates on their forms, and extra data can allow you to qualify and prioritize potential clients better. Collecting a first name also allows you to personalize your emails. Although again, the evidence on whether this results in increased email opens, clicks and sales is mixed. So it's something you might want to test yourself.

---

[10] See, for example, Copyblogger's description of their landing pages at http://www.copyblogger.com/email-landing-page/

One final tweak you can make is to the buttons on your opt-in forms. Usually, having the button text describe the benefit you'll get from subscribing (e.g. "Get Free Instant Access") results in higher opt-in rates than a button saying something like "Submit". And button colours that contrast with their surroundings tend to stick out and get clicked more than those that blend in. Again, only testing will show what works for you.

Decreasing Perceived Risk

The final factor that influences your opt-in rate is perceived risk. If your potential subscriber is worried that if they hand over their email address to sign up something bad will happen then they're much less likely to do so. Perhaps they fear getting spam from you or constant sales messages or that you'll sell their email address to someone else. In essence they don't trust you.

That impression is initially created by the look and feel of your website and what it says in and around the opt-in form. And it's quite market dependent. In some markets (the internet marketing field for example) having big scary bright red headlines that say 'warning' or that promise untold riches if you sign up are often given as examples of best practice. This could well be because in that kind of desperate market people really want to think that they're discovering secret formulas, things that Google is hiding from them and that they'll suddenly be able to make a lot of money overnight.

However, for most of us, our clients are not looking for a get rich quick scheme or for confirmation that the reason they're not successful is everyone else's fault. Sites and forms that look like that will discourage them from subscribing rather than encouraging them. So your first step is to make sure your site and your forms are in keeping with the expectations and look safe to your ideal clients. If they're conservative types, for example, you want a conservative looking website.

After that you can decrease the perceived risk by having a visible anti spam policy. You can include seals of approval from things like the Better Business Bureau or any professional associations you're a member of. You can include short quotes and testimonials from people (with permission) who already receive your emails saying how much they value them. All of that will decrease the perceived risk of signing up.

Perhaps the most powerful weapon here is social proof. Potential subscribers who don't know you probably don't believe you when you say how great your emails are and what value they're going to get from them. But if you include quotes and testimonials from current subscribers or customers saying what great value they get from your emails, then they'll tend to believe it. Especially if you include names and photographs.

Or once you've established a bit of a following simply quoting the total number of subscribers can create social proof. By saying, "Join 8,721 other subscribers who get daily client winning tips" for example; you're implying that there are a whole bunch of people who get value from your emails, so they should too.

Social proof works because most people are influenced, when they're faced with any kind of tricky choice, by what other people say and do. So if they're thinking of subscribing but they're a little bit uncertain then what could help push them over the edge is to see that lots of other people have done the same thing or people are seeing great things when they've subscribed and that's often enough to provide the impetus to get that many more subscribers.

For example, social media consultant Laura Roeder uses social proof to increase signups to her emails. By adding a quote saying, "Yours is the only newsletter that I actually read" to her opt-in form she increased sign ups by 24%. Adding the logos of the businesses she'd worked with came later and increased conversions even further.

Figure 14: Laura Roeder uses social proof to increase opt-ins

Summary

Getting permission by having subscribers actively opt-in is vital for effective email marketing. To maximize the number of people opting in to your emails you need to address the four key factors of the Opt-in formula:

- Maximising the perceived value subscribers will get from your emails.

- Creating an attractive incentive that helps subscribers address an immediate problem or goal.

- Minimising friction by making it as easy as possible for subscribers to opt-in and giving them plenty of opportunities to do so.

- Reducing perceived risk through a professional look and feel and by highlighting accreditations and social proof.

Your Next Steps

Review your current opt-in forms and landing pages (prioritize the ones with the most traffic and/or the worst opt-in rate). For each form or page, ask yourself the following questions:

- How can I describe the benefits of subscribing to my emails to increase their perceived value?

- What kind of incentive or lead magnet can I use to attract my ideal clients?

- How can I make my opt-in forms visible where my ideal clients are going on my site, reduce distractions, and make it as easy as possible for them to complete the forms?

- How can I make my ideal clients feel comfortable about subscribing and confident their information won't be abused?

3 READ ME: EFFECTIVE STRATEGIES TO GET YOUR EMAILS OPENED AND READ.

If you want your subscribers to take action on your emails, then three things need to happen:

- Your emails have to get through to them and not end up in spam folders or tabs on their email system that they don't read.

- They have to open up your emails.

- They have to read your emails to get to the call to action.

Getting Through to the Inbox

Your first challenge is to make sure your emails get through to your subscribers. You have to make sure they don't get classified as spam or get deprioritized and classed as "grey mail" (emails people have subscribed to, but don't seem interested in reading).

It used to be that keeping out of spam filters simply meant avoiding "trigger words" like *free* or *Rolex, credit card, Viagra*, or having dollar signs in your emails. You'll still often read advice on websites to avoid these words. And you'll even see emails from people who probably should know better with words like *f.ree* in them because they assume that if they used the word *free* their email would end up marked as spam.

Of course, spam filter algorithms are much more sophisticated than that and weigh up a whole series of factors. If it was simply a matter of changing a word or two, the spammers would have latched on to it years ago and we'd all be deluged with spam. As it is, most of us who use systems like Gmail or have our email filtered get very little spam these days.

Today's spam filter algorithms include technical factors like DKIM signatures and SPF records (don't worry, any reputable email system supplier will have these sorted out for you), the reputation of the email address and email system sending out the emails (i.e. whether they've previously been flagged as sending spam) and where the links in the emails go to (i.e. if they link to domains associated with previous spam reports).

They also, of course, take notice of how many times your emails get flagged as spam by subscribers. One of the biggest causes of this is a mismatch between what a subscriber expects when they sign up, and what you send them. So make sure that when they're signing up you tell them how often you'll be mailing them and what about. I explicitly tell my subscribers that since I make my money by selling training courses and coaching, they'll occasionally receive promotional emails from me so that they're not surprised when they do.

Make sure you stay "on topic". If your subscribers signed up for emails about cost reduction and you start sending them material on marketing then even though you're certain it would be valuable for them, it's not what they're expecting.

According to Brendan Dubbels, head of deliverability at email system provider Ontraport and responsible for getting over one and a half billion emails delivered per year, the big emerging factor in email deliverability is "engagement".

The more your subscribers open your emails, the more time they spend reading them, scrolling down them, replying to them or clicking links in them, the more likely it is that future emails from you will stay out of the spam folder.

The big email services like Hotmail and Gmail (which also runs a lot of corporate email systems behind the scenes) are also using community based metrics. So not only does the engagement level of an individual subscriber impact whether future emails from you will end up in his or her spam folder, it also impacts how likely your emails are to end up in the spam folders of all other subscribers on using that email system. According to Dubbels, Hotmail even goes as far as retrospectively "fishing unread emails out of the inbox and putting them in spam if a lot of users start flagging them".

The same engagement and community level metrics apply to a new phenomenon: greymail.

Greymail is Hotmail's terminology for email newsletters and other emails that people sign up for, but end up rarely reading. In the past, unread newsletters would just clog up a users inbox. Today, email providers are giving them tools to automatically shift them to lower priority folders or to unsubscribe from multiple newsletters en masse. Gmail's introduction of a tabbed inbox with a tab for promotional emails (that most email newsletters end up in by default instead of the main inbox) is just the latest in a series of moves designed to help email users make sense of their inbox. The side effect is that even if your emails don't end up in spam, your subscribers still might not see them.

The route out of greymail, as with spam, is engagement. The more your subscribers actually open and read your emails and take action on them, the less likely they are to end up deprioritized. If your emails have great content and are enjoyable to read, then your subscribers will drag them out of the promotional tab on Gmail and into their main inbox without you having to beg them to do so.

And since engagement metrics work on percentages, "list hygiene" is becoming increasingly important. This means that if your email list contains a large number of subscribers who aren't opening or acting on your emails, you're better off removing them from the list (after a reminder email or two) so that you have a high percentage of action takers per email.

According to Dubbels, a number of Ontraport users have found that when they cleaned up their lists, not only did they get higher open and click *percentages*, they got a higher *absolute number* of opens, clicks and most importantly sales as their emails got into inboxes they hadn't previously.

Most email systems have analysis tools that will report if your emails have too many suspicious words in them, or use too many images compared to the amount of text (an old trick used by spammers to try to fool spam detection systems by putting everything in images that the systems couldn't read).

If you use those tools, keep your email lists clean, deliver useful and entertaining content in your emails and encourage subscribers to interact with you by clicking and replying; then you shouldn't have too much of a problem with getting your email delivered.

Double or Single Opt-in?

One of the great debates in email marketing is whether you should use a double opt-in process or single opt-in.

Double opt-in means that after a subscriber has completed an opt-in form they're sent an email and asked to confirm that they want to receive regular emails from you by clicking a link. With single opt-in they just start getting your emails.

Email marketing system providers prefer you to use double opt-in. It protects them from rogue marketers using their system to add names of people who haven't granted permission to be emailed. And it provides an audit trail for them so if any subscribers complain, they can point to the exact moment when they confirmed they wanted the emails.

Figure 15: A typical double opt-in confirmation email

The benefits for the business or individual sending the emails aren't so clear cut. On the one hand, you could argue that since people have confirmed they want your emails they're more qualified: they've gone an extra step to ask for them. But on the other hand, what you're doing with double opt-in is asking people who've already asked for something to ask for it again. Apart from being annoying, a certain percentage just won't see or go through with the confirmation request, especially if they're not used to the process of confirming.

A client of mine recently told me that his opt-ins doubled when he switched to single opt-in. Now that may be an extreme case, but it illustrates that you need to make a balanced decision on double or single opt-in.

One advantage of double opt-in on some email marketing systems is that double opted-in emails get sent from a different server to single opted-in emails. In that case your emails are less likely to be sent from the same server as someone who might abuse the system and so they're less likely to get stuck in spam filters. Not every email marketing system does this, so check with yours.

So while double opt-in is the safest bet for many people, I personally use single opt-in. I get close to zero spam reports (everyone gets some, even if it's just because it's easier to hit the spam button than to click to unsubscribe). And I'm not in the sort of market where a vicious competitor would subscribe unwilling people to my emails just to hit me with spam reports. So by doing single opt-in I don't ask my subscribers to jump through an extra hoop just to get what they've already asked for. I do, however, keep my list clean by removing people who don't open or click emails for months.

Getting Your Emails Opened

First a caveat: your primary goal is *not* to get your emails opened. It's to get your subscribers to take action. So your ultimate measure of whether your emails are working should be your sales or contact form submissions or other actions you're looking for them to take, not your email open rate. It's not unknown for your open rates to go down, but your sales to go up because you hit on the right email for your real buyers rather than just passive readers who didn't open up the email this time.

So throughout this section bear in mind that we're not just looking to get subscribers to open our emails. We're looking to get the right subscribers, those ready to take action, to open and ideally to prime them to take that action.

The biggest factor, in my experience, in whether a subscriber will open your email or not is nothing to do with the email itself, it's who the email is sent from.

Sender Reputation

If you think about it, if you receive an email from your husband or wife, friend or lover or best business contacts, you open them up no matter what time of day or night or what the subject line says. You know in advance that whatever's in that email is going to be worth reading.

Ideally you want to reach the same position yourself. And the key is to build a reputation for delivering great value in the first few emails you send. If your lead magnet delivers tremendous insights then your initial emails will be opened with positive anticipation. If they hit the spot, if they're a useful and entertaining read, then your name will be mentally tagged as one of those people whose emails they'll try to open whenever they can. So opening emails from you becomes a habit.

You can go a step further, too. If you encourage your subscribers to take action on your emails, like asking you a question by replying to your emails or completing a survey or sharing something on social media, then taking action becomes a habit. And if those actions result in them getting a reward of some sort; so if you reply personally to their questions or they get a free gift for completing the survey, then they'll associate opening your emails and taking action with positive things happening for them and they'll keep on doing it.

Obviously, for this strategy to work, you need your emails to consistently come from the same "from" address – ideally your name or the name of a member of your staff. Try not to send emails from info@businessname.com or worse still donotreply@businessname.com. That tells your subscriber that you're a faceless corporation or marketing department and you're not really interested in hearing from them.

Email Subject Lines That Get Subscribers to Open Your Emails

After your name and reputation the next key factor that determines whether subscribers will open your email is the subject line. Decades ago, copywriter Gary Bencivenga came up with the following formula for writing advertising headlines:

$$I = B + C$$

Or in plain English: Interest = Benefits + Curiosity.

The same holds true for your email subject lines. People are going to be motivated to open emails that promise something useful. But if they think they already know what's going to be in the email, they'll skip it, especially if they're short of time. So you need both benefits and curiosity in an ideal email subject line.

Some example from my own emails on winning more clients:

- *The Real Secrets of Linkedin*. Benefits = learn to use Linkedin better. Curiosity = "just what are the real secrets?"

- *How I Increased Email Signups by 51%*. Benefits = get more email signups. Curiosity = "what on earth did Ian do to get such a big increase?"

- *Why Honey Nut Cheerios get more word of mouth than Disney World*. Benefit = learn how to get more word of mouth. Curiosity = "why would something as mundane as Cheerios get more word of mouth than something as amazing as Disney World?"

- *5 crippling beliefs that keep consultants and coaches in the poor house.* Benefit = avoid those beliefs yourself. Curiosity = "I wonder what they are? And I hope I don't have them!"

How do you come up with benefits? You head back to your customer insight map and look at all the goals and aspirations, problems and issues that you've identified your ideal clients have. That should give you quite a long list of different topics that you could potentially write about. Take that list of topics and expand on it. Drill into some of them in more detail. There could be two, three, four, five points on each individual topic that you could write an email and an interesting subject line for.

So for example if you're in the field of leadership and one of the topics that your client struggles with is their own self-confidence then in terms of expanding that topic there could be something on the causes of a lack of self-confidence. There could be three or four on different ways of overcoming a lack of self-confidence. There could be two or three case studies you might have from your own experience about working with clients who have overcome self-confidence issues. There could be half a dozen different examples of people who have suffered from a lack of self-confidence in the public eye. Film stars, TV entertainers, rock legends or sportspeople who have suffered and you can tell their story. Or emails that show why common accepted wisdom on self-confidence is wrong, why doing nothing is not an option, or the "dirty little secrets" of self confident people.

You can expand those original topics from your customer insight map by brainstorming or mind mapping to turn each one into five, six or more individual sub-topics that could form the basis of an email, each one of which would be interesting to your potential clients.

You can then add curiosity to the subject line in a number of ways:

- Pulling out something surprising about the topic or disagreeing with conventional wisdom. E.g. *Why improving your selling skills will lose you sales.*

- Adding some form of quantification or ranking. E.g. *The top 3 reasons you're losing sales.* In this case curiosity is aroused because subscribers want to find out what you think are the top 3 reasons and whether they agree with them.

- Harnessing an emotion. E.g. *7 ways big corporates try to stop you succeeding.* In this case tapping in to potential anger and suspicion about large corporates.

- Linking the topic to something unexpected. E.g. *What Jeremy Clarkson taught me about marketing.* The curiosity is in wanting to know what a TV celebrity could know about a topic they're not usually associated with.

- Hooking in to news and current affairs. E.g. *How to achieve Olympic performance in your organisation.* Health warning: these can often go stale fast, especially if lots of people make the same analogies. If you're linking to the news, try to make it a less common story or come at it from an angle no one else is using.

- Name drop a known expert in your field. E.g. *David Ogilvy's best performing adverts.* People are curious to see behind the scenes of what a well-known industry expert thinks and does.

- Admit your mistakes. E.g. *My WORST sales meeting ever.* A mixture of wanting to know what to avoid themselves and a little schadenfreude at hearing what you did wrong means these emails often get a very high open rate.

In terms of then writing the subject lines, often your completely original ones will work best as they'll be in your natural voice. But if you're short of inspiration, then building on a tried and tested headline formula like the following can help:

The How To Model

- How to <achieve benefit>

- How to <achieve benefit> even if <common barrier>

- How to <achieve benefit> in less than <time period>

The Surprising Link Model

- What I learned about <topic> from <surprising person>

- <surprising person>'s guide to <topic>

The List Model

- <number> ways to <do something useful>

- <number> surprising facts about <topic>

- The top <number> reasons you're <something bad>

The Secrets Model

- <number> secret ways to <do something good>

- What your <person in authority> doesn't want you to know about <something in their field>

The Questions Model

- What would happen if you <big change/achievement>?

- Has <problem> ever happened to you?

- Do you know the top reason why <something good/bad> happens?

The Unusual Sentence Model
- "<surprising quote>" (e.g. "You're fired, Mr Peesker")
- <really unexpected sentence> (e.g. Dripping blood, sponges and something that may be holding you back)

Finding the Right Subject Line for *Your* Audience

Effective subject lines are one of the things that vary considerably by audience and are often difficult to predict. Some marketers have reported very high open rates with subject lines like "Hey!", "Open Up" and "Bad News!". These are the sort of tricks that work for a while until everyone starts using them, or until your subscribers get wise and realize you're just trying to trick them into opening an email that bears no relation to the subject line. Best to stick to subjects that give a good idea of what's in the email while still invoking curiosity.

Try not to overuse specific subject line models. If all your emails are "How To..." or link an aspect of your business with a celebrity then eventually they become a bit predictable. Add variety to your emails by using a different model each time so that by the time you repeat a model it's been long enough for it to seem fresh again.

And if you're going to be using a specific email repeatedly (for example if it's a standard email that all subscribers get as part of an autoresponder sequence) then consider split testing different subject lines to see which one performs best, then use that one in the sequence.

And, of course, you won't be able to come up with a killer subject line every time. That's why it's important to build up a great reputation with your subscribers so they open your emails regardless of whether they have a brilliant subject line or not.

Writing Emails "In Reverse"

So far I've described choosing and writing email subject lines as a very logical process starting with the client benefit or problem and then trying to find an interesting hook for it. In practice, however, it often happens the other way around.

When email marketing becomes a habit for you, you'll find that you begin to notice interesting topics for emails in your daily life. Something in a book you read or in the news or that you spot on an early morning walk triggers your interest and you think it would make a good hook or story for an email. You then "backfill" to try to find a way of linking that interesting hook to a client benefit or problem you can talk about.

I got an email from a client of mine recently for example. He'd seen an excellent performance from a comedy magician at the Edinburgh Fringe the evening before and thought it would make a great hook for an email, but was struggling to link it to a useful topic for his clients.

The way to proceed here is simply to list all the things you found interesting in what you saw and you'll often find that a link to a useful topic jumps off the page at you. In this case he identified that the magician chose his audience helpers well (always a pretty girl) and that although he was impressed by the skill of the magician, the thing that made the performance was the way he built rapport with the audience through comedy.

This lead him to realize that he could write an email about how success for his clients was more determined by their people skills than by their technical skills. A simple point, but made interesting by the magician analogy.

The First Few Lines Can Make a Difference

These days many email browsers not only show the subject line of an email in your inbox, they also show the first line or so of the email. So the first few lines of the email are almost like mini subject lines themselves in that what they say can encourage a subscriber to click and open up the email to read it all.

So if your email begins with something boring like "Dear Friend" or the standard "If you can't read this email click here to read it online" message that some email systems add automatically to the top of emails, then that's not going to encourage subscribers to read it.

If however the first line of your email is something they would be interested in just like a subject line, then that can also increase the chances of the email being opened.

For example, if your subject line of your email is something like, 'My Worst Sales Meeting Ever' and people are opening the email to find out how to improve their own sales meetings and a bit of curiosity to find out what your worst sales meeting was like, then you could open the email by saying, "Holding successful sales meetings is critical to the success of your business. Here's where I got it badly wrong and what you can learn to improve the effectiveness of your sales meetings."

So in that case you're introducing the story but you're also telling them why reading this email will be beneficial to them. Or, you could get them thinking by asking a question. So again with that 'My Worst Sales Meeting Ever' email, you could say, "Have you ever had a really bad sales meeting?" And that question will trigger their thinking and build a bit of empathy and then you can go on to describe your worst ever sales meeting. Or you could combine them both. You can say, "Have you ever had a really bad sales meeting?

Getting sales meetings right is incredibly important, but it's easy for them to go wrong. Here's an example of my worst ever sales meeting and what you can learn to improve the effectiveness of yours."

So the idea with each of these opening sentences is that after they've clicked on the email to open it, you're then drawing them in to the body of the email, you're re-stressing how useful and interesting it's going to be to read on.

First Impressions Count

After an email has been opened, there's another very short phase that happens before your subscriber will read it. And it's a critical but much overlooked one.

As soon as the email is opened, your reader will take in an *overall impression* of the email, and in particular:

- Whether the email looks like a commercial or promotional email (usually if there are lots of graphics and images in it and big headlines), and...

- Whether the email looks easy to read.

This latter point is particularly important if the email is opened on a mobile device. It's difficult enough for most people to read the small fonts in emails on an iPhone or Blackberry, but if the email looks dense, with long sentences and paragraphs, then the reader will often close it again quickly and plan to come back to it later (and of course, usually won't).

Worse still, some email systems send out emails that don't render properly on mobile devices. They use desktop-formatted images in the headers and footers of emails which cause the mobile device to shrink the email to fit in the screen. This makes the text appear tiny by default and requires the reader to zoom in and pan left and right to have any chance of reading the email. In practice, they don't, it's too painful. They close it and move on.

So make sure your emails are mobile friendly and can be easily read on small screens. That means plenty of white space with short sentences and paragraphs that make them look easily digestible when opened up. Even long emails can be made to look easy-to-read by the judicious use of white space and formatting.

Personally, I like to send relatively short emails: 300-500 words where possible. If I need to say more on a topic I'd rather send multiple, easy-to-read emails spread over a few days than one long, difficult-to-read email that gets ignored.

Timing Your Emails to Get More Opens and Clicks

One of the questions I often get asked when I'm running a training session on email marketing is "when's the best day or time to send emails?". And like many email related topics, the true answer is that it depends on your audience. If your ideal clients work in a job where they're out in the field all day and can't pick up emails then an early morning or late evening email is more likely to get through to them while they're actively working through their inbox. Business owners may be frantically processing only the most urgent emails during the week, but have more time to digest your emails over the weekend.

So again, it's only by testing what works for your audience that you find the real answer for you. There are, however, some general statistics and trends available.

Dan Zarrella, author of *The Science of Marketing*[11] analysed data from over 9 billion emails sent by MailChimp. He discovered that the Click Through Rate (the percentage of emails where the reader clicked a link in the email) was the highest for emails sent over the weekend.

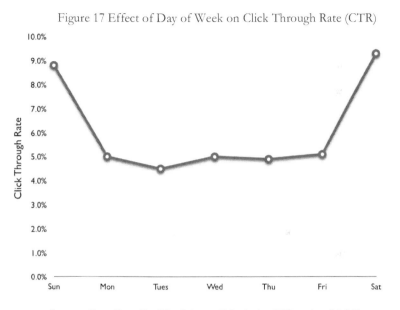

Figure 17 Effect of Day of Week on Click Through Rate (CTR)

Source: Dan Zarrella, *The Science of Marketing*, Wiley, April 2013.

This is part of a wider phenomenon Zarrella calls "Contra-Competitive Timing". When it comes to emails, tweets or blog posts, you're more likely to get attention if you send yours when there's less competition for airtime.

Similarly, the best time of day to send emails seems to be very early in the morning so that they're the first thing in your subscribers' inbox when they get to work before emails from colleagues, customers and suppliers start piling in.

---

[11] Dan Zarrella, *The Science of Marketing: When to Tweet, What to Post, How to Blog, and Other Proven Strategies*, Wiley, April 2013.

Based on this data, I try to email early in the morning or at the weekend whenever I can. However I don't let a quest for perfect timing cause me to hesitate or significantly delay sending emails out. And if everyone reads Zarrella's findings then weekends and mornings will become crowded rather than Contra-Competitive and they'll lose their effectiveness.

Figure 18 Effect of Time of Day on Click Through Rate

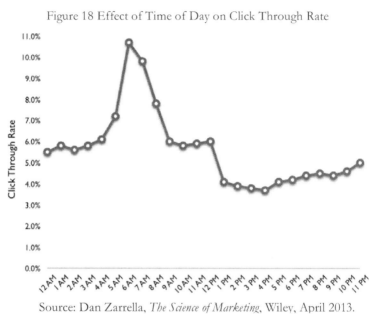

Source: Dan Zarrella, *The Science of Marketing*, Wiley, April 2013.

The Final timing factor that will affect the success of your emails is frequency: how often you send out emails.

Many surveys have been done on email frequency with respondents regularly saying that one of the main reasons they unsubscribe from emails is that they get sent too many. The data, however, tells a different story. When Zarrella looked at unsubscribe rates and click rates for different frequencies of emails he found that:

- Unsubscribe rates were higher for less frequently emailed lists than frequently mailed ones (rates falling from 0.7% for lists emailed once a month to 0.15% for lists mailed daily)

- Click rates decreased very little as email frequency increased, going down from around 6% per email for lists mailed once or twice per month to 5% per email for those emailed daily. And since the rate is per email, the daily emails generated over 20 times as many clicks overall.

Zarrella's conclusion was that "sending more email is not the marketing taboo many of us had thought it to be. As long as you're following the guidelines set forth in the rest of this chapter and sending targeted, personalized and value-packed emails, sending more of them is better".

Frequent communications across all walks of business and life are a sign of close relationships. Yes, sending emails daily or three or four times a week will be too many for some people. But if you're genuinely sending useful, interesting emails each time then those people who can't invest a few minutes a day to read them are unlikely to form a close enough relationship with you to become a valuable client.

When you're deciding on timing and frequency for your emails, you may not be able to manage daily emails, but you should try to email as often as possible as long as you can maintain a high level of quality.

Summary

The key to getting subscribers to open and read your email lies in five main factors:

1. Making sure your emails get through spam and greymail filters by keeping them on topic and high value.

2. Quickly establishing a reputation for sending valuable, entertaining emails that your subscribers want to read so that opening your emails becomes a habit.

3. Using subject lines which promise benefits and invoke curiosity and following that up in the first few lines of the email.

4. Making sure your emails look easy to read across all devices.

5. Sending your emails when your subscribers are likely to have less in their inbox.

Your Next Steps

Review the emails you're sending to subscribers – especially the early ones – to ensure:

- They have benefit focused subject lines that where possible invoke curiosity. Try reworking your subject lines using the guidelines and formulas in this chapter to increase their impact.

- They make a positive impression early on. "Front load" your best emails that deliver the most value and are the most interesting by putting them early in your interactions with a subscriber so that they come to expect great stuff from you.

- They're easy to read. Use short sentences and paragraphs along with plenty of white space. Check how your emails look on the main mobile devices: iPhones, Android phones and iPads. You can either use an actual device to check, or the free email format checking service provided by Litmus at https://litmus.com/email-testing.

- Test sending emails over the weekend, early in the morning or late at night to see the impact on how often they're opened and read (read the chapter on measuring and testing for more details on how).

4 TALK TO ME: WRITING EMAILS THAT ENGAGE AND PERSUADE.

"Engagement" has become a bit of a buzzword recently and it's running the risk of just becoming a synonym for "good". So let's talk about what we mean by it.

And let's start with the context that our overall goal is for our email subscribers to take action. Usually buying a product from us or hiring us to perform a service. So engagement is a means to that end.

In that context, engagement with your email subscribers is where:

- They believe they have a relationship with you over and above just being recipients of your emails. They trust you and they believe in the value of what you do.

- They take action on your emails over and above just reading them. This can vary from simply forwarding them on to friends, sharing or liking blog posts, completing surveys, hitting reply to ask or answer a question, right through to interacting with you in depth over email, phone or even in person.

What we're aiming to do is get our subscribers used to taking action whenever we send them an email. If subscribers see themselves as action takers when they receive your emails because they've taken small actions before, then when they're considering a bigger action like calling you to discuss working together or buying one of your products, they're much more likely to do it.

We're also building our relationship with them by interacting personally. The more your subscribers interact with you and get good things from you, the more they'll like you and be willing to do things for you.

In many ways, email marketing is like a romantic relationship. You meet, which is the equivalent of your email subscriber opting in to receive emails from you. Over time you want to build a relationship with that special person, so you might send them chocolates, you might send them flowers, you might invite them out to the cinema.

The problem is, if you're the only one sending gifts or being nice to the other person and they're just eating the chocolates, putting the flowers in a vase and never doing anything for you in return then you're not really building any kind of relationship at all. Certainly not one that's going to end up in a long-term commitment.

It's the same with email marketing, if you're regularly sending useful, valuable information to people and they're just reading it but never acting on it, never doing anything as a result, never interacting with you, then your relationship isn't really building. You may be establishing some basic level of credibility but you're not really building a relationship.

As a result, what then happens is when you want them to take a bigger action, like to buy a product from you or to give you a phone call to talk about working together, it's a very big step for them because they've never really engaged or acted on any of your emails before.

By contrast, if they are engaging with your emails and acting on them, then when you ask them to take a bigger action they're much more ready to take that step because they've already taken smaller steps and they've had good results from taking those smaller steps.

Three Steps to Engagement

In order to engage with your subscribers through your emails you need to do three things:

- Firstly, you need to speak to them in a way that's personal and different to the way they're normally marketed to by faceless corporations.

- Secondly, you need to communicate with them in ways that go beyond merely regurgitating facts and figures, hints and tips. You need to entertain as well as inform.

- Thirdly, you need to ask them to take action and make it easy for them to do so.

Establishing Your Character

Most business emails we get are dull, dull, dull. And they're sent to us by people who seem to have no wish to connect with us as human beings. They either just want to tell us what their latest offers are, or give us dry "content" that's supposed to build their credibility.

And while we may subscribe and open up emails because they offer us useful information, we stay subscribed and we keep reading because of something more.

Most successful email marketers have a clearly defined character. A personality they project in their emails.

When I receive emails from veteran direct marketer Drayton Bird (the man David Ogilvy said knew more about direct marketing than anyone else in the world), it feels like I'm being written to by a cantankerous uncle. Simultaneously angry, funny, and full of worldly wisdom based on years of hard won experience.

Bnonn Tennant sends emails that feel to all the world like they've been written by a slightly weird, geeky older brother. A guy with a huge vocabulary and a keen insight into business, but who seems more interested in video games and archery.

Many marketers, especially those in professional advisory roles like business coaches, consultant or lawyers, adopt a "trusted business friend" character. They write to you in the casual style you'd expect from a long-standing mentor or senior colleague. Yet all of them have their unique twists too.

Dov Gordon, for example, projects an image of a deep thinker. Someone obsessed with simplifying the complex and solving the trickiest problems. Danny Iny is a man on a mission to spread the word of ethical online business and the huge opportunities for entrepreneurs to get their message across via the web. Steve Gordon is a practical hands-on guy who's sharing the experience he's had himself and through his successful clients.

By adopting a distinct character, you can differentiate yourself from the vast majority of the people who'll be emailing your subscribers. You'll be more memorable, and your strengths will be noted more keenly.

To figure out what your email character could be, make a list of what you believe your key strengths to be, why your potential clients would value these, and examples and stories you can tell to illustrate these strengths.

In my own case, I identified my background as someone who wasn't a natural at marketing and selling as something my ideal clients could empathize with, along with a very practical nature, openness and transparency and a sense of humour and willingness to share my failings as well as my successes.

When I write emails, that's the version of me that I'd like to come across to subscribers. It implies that I need to write quite casually; I need to tell stories about my past and show how I learned marketing and sales, including my failures and stumbles along the way. I need to inject a bit of humour or light-heartedness into my emails.

This is an area where individuals and small businesses have a tremendous advantage over larger businesses. By building a personal connection and emailing as a real human being rather than using corporate or marketing-speak you're much more likely to stand out, be likable, and to make an impact.

Don't worry if your character isn't fully formed when you first start emailing. Just focus on a few key areas that you feel comfortable with. If you're relaxed about writing emails (a topic we'll come on to shortly), then your personality will gradually emerge over time.

Writing Conversationally

By and large, for most types of character, a conversational and informal tone is the best to adopt when you're writing emails. Write your email as if you were speaking. If you imagine your ideal client sitting with you over a coffee, or perhaps a beer in a bar, and you're just chatting to them. Try to write in the same tone of voice you would use for that chat. That will establish that friendly, advisory relationship that you're trying to set up with them.

For a casual chat you wouldn't talk formally as if you were lecturing them. You wouldn't talk in business or corporate speak with all sorts of jargon in it and long complex words just to try to sound clever. You wouldn't speak as if you were addressing a group and use phrases like "some of you" or "you guys". You'd talk person-to-person. Informally.

If you're used to writing formally, it can take a little bit of time before you relax and get comfortable writing more conversationally. But the more emails and blog posts you write, the more comfortable you'll get with this style and the easier it'll become until it becomes the natural style that you write in.

I also advise that when it comes to the look and feel of your emails, to keep them as simple as possible. You want to mimic the style of email that your character would genuinely send. So a trusted business colleague, a cantankerous uncle or geeky older brother wouldn't send a fancy formatted email with headers, logos and five different articles in it. They'd send fairly plain emails with maybe a bit of bolding and underlining and some links. And they'd focus on one thing at a time.

When marketingexperiments.com studied click through rates for different types of email a few years ago, they came to a very similar conclusion[12]. They discovered that emails that use a lot of graphics and formatting got 34% fewer clicks than plain text emails.

But emails that had a little bit of formatting: the occasional underline, or bolded text, or links highlighted in the normal colour for links; they got 55% more clicks than plain text.

---

[12] Data reported by email marketing provider Aweber in their blog post "Text vs. HTML: Is Moderation the Key?".

For me, the reason is that lightly formatted emails look like the emails we get from people we know and trust: our friends, our business colleagues, our advisors, our clients. Graphics heavy emails look like the emails we get from retailers and people trying to sell us something, so we automatically put up our barriers.

And as we said before, graphics can play havoc with mobile devices causing them to shrink down the text and make it almost unreadable.

Now, this is one of those areas that really does differ depending on your target audience and needs to be tested. Many people *say* they like to receive graphics in emails but their behaviour indicates that they actually click more and pay more attention when the emails are fairly simple.

Inform AND Entertain

This is one of the most important but underused strategies for engaging with your readers.

As Bnonn Tennant puts it, "they sign up for the content. But they stay and they keep reading for the entertainment".

Fiction books have always outsold non-fiction. The best-selling book in the UK in 2012 was EL James' *Fifty Shades of Grey*, selling a whopping 4,457,021 copies according to The Guardian, nearly ten times as many copies as the best-selling non-fiction book, Jamie Oliver's *15 Minute Meals* recipe book.

On TV, soap operas and crime dramas are the regular staples we tune in to week in, week out rather than documentaries. And even the most popular "serious" shows often get their following based on how entertainingly they can present their material. Witness the success of *Mythbusters*, or the revitalisation of *The Sky At Night* with Brian Cox as presenter.

That's not to say that you need to become a world-class fiction writer to run effective email campaigns. But you can learn to use some of the tools and techniques of fiction to make your emails more engaging.

In particular, what almost every successful TV or radio show, book or play has is **human interest**. We care much more about people than we do about facts and figures. That's why, these days, when charities want us to donate then instead of sending us information about the huge scale of poverty they're dealing with or the number of distressed animals they're helping, they tell us a story about one child who's lost his parents and is having to bring up his family at the age of 11 and walks ten miles to the well for water every morning. Or one mistreated dog who's now found a loving home thanks to previous donations to the charity.

In your emails, instead of just writing about your topics, tell a story that illustrates your points. Many of my emails are stories about marketing and sales problems I've encountered myself and lessons I've learned that will be helpful to my readers. Or you can write about your clients and the work you've done with them. The *Surprising Link* model for emails lends itself naturally to writing about someone famous or interesting.

It doesn't have to be complex. Sometimes the very best story emails work like fables or parables. They use an analogy to let the reader draw their own conclusions and extract their own insights. This can be much more powerful than spelling out the details as the insight will be much more meaningful to the individual reader.

My very first story-based email was called "So, are you going to do this..." It told the story of how when my wife Kathy and I moved into our dream home back in 1994 we discovered that the plot of land at the bottom of the garden we'd earmarked for my vegetable patch actually had a whole load of rubbish (including a three foot high brick wall) buried in it. So for year after year I put off clearing it out as it just seemed like a lot of work. Eventually, Kathy said to me "so, are you going to do this..." and we knuckled down over a couple of back-breaking weekends to clear it and plant the garden.

The point – that sometimes in life you just have to knuckle down and do the hard work to get what you want – is a simple one. And because it was so simple and didn't include any of the detailed marketing hints and tips I'd been including in previous emails I was worried that it wouldn't go down well.

But shortly after I sent it I started getting emails back from people telling me how it really resonated with them. How they'd had a similar experience. Or how it had made them realize they needed to do the same to make progress on their big goals.

It helped form a human connection with my readers, too. I wasn't the all-conquering hero of the story. I was the fallible person who'd put off a tough task for years. So it helped readers see that I wasn't some super productive iron willed marketing expert who could do things they couldn't do. If I could do something, so could they.

Your stories don't have to be particularly complex. The story element of Danny Iny's emails is often just in the introduction as he describes why the particular topic his email is about is important. It's often as simple as mentioning the name of the person who's sent him in a question and stating why they asked it and how it impacts their business. Simple though it is, that's enough to give a human-interest element to his emails and make them more interesting.

At the other extreme, copywriter Daniel Levis plots entire campaigns of emails using classic storytelling techniques. He defines who the protagonist and antagonist in each email will be, creates a plot in the time-tested narrative structure of problem-complication-resolution, and identifies the emotions he's trying to harness in each email.

That may sound like a lot of work, but since Daniel specializes in focused sales email campaigns, the bottom line impact makes that investment well worth it.

Most effective email writers will tie their story in to a piece of content or useful information they're getting across to their reader. But you needn't always make a serious point in every email. Going back to Bnonn Tennant and his comment that your subscribers stay for the entertainment; sometimes that's enough in its own right. Raise a smile and you've done your job for the day.

In similar vein Kristina Mand-Lakhiani, CEO of publishing powerhouse MindValley Russia stresses the need to send out a "balanced diet" of emails to your subscribers. In their mind-body-spirit niche they try to send a mix of content emails that share useful information, engagement emails where they ask their readers to do something, sales emails where they promote their products, and inspirational emails where they share case studies or thoughts designed to give their readers the self-belief and confidence to succeed.

Asking for Action

Establishing a clear persona, writing conversationally and building human interest into your emails are all techniques for building a more personal relationship with your readers. And that means they're much more likely to take action on your emails.

The next big secret to getting people to engage and take action on your emails is *simply to ask them*.

If you're writing to them personally so they feel like they know you, and if they've got value from your lead magnet and the emails they've read so far then they'll often feel they "owe you one". At least enough to take a small step. Then if you make it simple for them to take that action and there's a reason why you're asking, then you're very likely to get them to respond.

Early on, make sure you're asking your readers for things that are simple and relatively easy to do with a logical reason why this would be helpful for you and them. So you might ask them to complete a short survey on a specific topic and the reason may be to help you create some free training material for them downstream.

You can use something like SurveyMonkey or Google Forms. If there are just two, three, or four questions that they can complete in just a couple of minutes then you'll get a good response. Or you may ask them to just hit reply to your email and tell you what their priorities are right now, with the reason that it'll help you understand what to focus your future emails on.

You may have written a short report that you want to give away in future, so you can give your readers a preview of it and ask for their feedback. Or even just say something along the lines of "I'm working on writing a book this weekend, I'm thinking of making the title this..., I'm thinking of covering these topics..." And get their feedback on it.

Or you could ask them to connect with you on LinkedIn, or Facebook or follow you on Twitter or ask them to like a video or an article on your webpage.

These are all small steps, but you're getting your readers into more of a two-way relationship with you. Going back to the romance analogy it's progressing from you just sending gifts to them reciprocating.

One particularly powerful strategy is simply to ask your readers to reply to an email. This could be to get feedback as we've mentioned above. Or you could do what MindValley do and after you've sent new subscribers an email with a link to download the lead magnet they signed up for, send them an email asking them to hit reply and just say "yes" if they were able to download it.

Not only does this give your readers an easy action they can take, it gives you the opportunity to email them back and to strike up a one-to-one dialogue with them. Not everyone will reply, and not everyone will then respond when you email back personally. But those that do will have a much closer bond with you than with any other marketers who are sending them emails that they just passively read.

Here's an example of how Danny Iny used this strategy to great effect. He arranged to do a guest article for one of the writers of a syndicated blog on the online site of Forbes magazine. After the blog had been published he sent an email to his subscribers telling them that he'd written the guest post, how excited he was about it since it was the biggest site he'd written for and asking them politely, if they could, to click through and read the article and ideally to comment on it, give him feedback on it, and if possible to share it on social media.

A few days later he sent another email giving his subscribers an update and reporting that the article had already been viewed many thousands of times and that if he could get more comments and shares the article could end up on the home page of Forbes.

Again, Danny's readers took action and he sent a third email to thank them and to report that the article had indeed made it onto the home page of Forbes as the second most popular article of the week.

If we look at what Danny did, he phrased his request so that it didn't come across as too self-serving. He talked about wanting to get the article out, share it with people and help people through it. And he asked for feedback and comments to help him improve.

But importantly, he wasn't afraid to ask for a favour. He'd been sending people great material through his emails, so it was only fair that he should ask a favour in return. Then once people had done that action for him, he thanked them for helping and told them what had happened.

What he did was enrol his readers in a joint project they did together. It was all about 'we' rather than just about him. They worked on getting the article popular together, and they were rewarded by hearing updates about its progress and shared in the success when it made it to the home page.

So as a result of his emails, his readers felt as if they'd done something successful with him and were much more likely to do something again for him when asked. Including attending webinars or eventually, buying one of his products.

That's the kind of engagement that means something. And it's the kind of engagement you can get if you follow the three steps of establishing a persona, writing conversationally and using stories, and suggesting your readers take small actions that give them positive outcomes.

Structuring Your Emails

As you get more experienced at writing emails the structure will naturally flow from your subject line and "lead" (the first few paragraphs) to your call to action at the end. When you're just starting though, it can be helpful to try to structure your emails according to the time-tested AIDA formula.

AIDA is an acronym for the different things you need to do in an effective piece of advertising or sales letter. But it works just as well for your emails.

A is for Attention. You've got to grab the attention of your potential reader otherwise they just won't read your email. You do this with an effective subject line as we've already discussed.

I is for Interest. Now that you've got their attention you need to get them interested enough that they'll read the full email. You could do that by expanding on the benefits (i.e. showing what they'll learn from the email and why it's important). Or you could play up the curiosity angle. Start with a dramatic story-based opening: "I'd just made the biggest business mistake of my life and was faced with a stark choice: either soldier on and hope that eventually sales would recover, or give up, take a huge hit, and start again…". Who wouldn't want to read on to find out what happened?

You can begin emails with compelling facts, by asking questions, or stating something shocking. Either way, you need to ask yourself "if my ideal client read the first few lines of this email, would they get interested enough to read the rest of the email?".

D is for Desire. In advertising your goal is to build desire to buy your product by highlighting its benefits. In an email you're usually going to be less overtly sales focused. You're going to deliver the payoff to your initial promise: tell the story, give them useful information, introduce some new ideas. But don't forget that in doing so you still want to motivate your readers to take action. To click the link at the end of your email, hit reply, forward it on: whatever action you want. We cover this in depth in the next chapters, but always ask yourself: "does the body of my email not only deliver what I promised, but also build desire to take action?".

Finally, **A is for Action**. After reading your email you want your readers to take action. It may be something small like clicking through to read a blog post or watch a video. It may be to hit reply and ask you a question or to complete a survey. Ultimately you'd like them to do something like buying a product or asking to speak to you about working together. Again, more on this in the following chapters, but structure-wise: make sure your email has a clear call to action.

Summary

The goal of engagement is to build a relationship with your subscribers so that they're ready and willing to take the actions you're looking for (for example to buy a product or book a 1-1 call with you).

To achieve that, your emails need to speak to them personally. Write conversationally from a defined character, tell stories with human interest, entertain as well as inform. Ask them to take small actions at first that provide positive results for them like completing a survey to help you tailor the contents of upcoming emails. The more your subscribers get used to taking action when they receive an email from you and the more benefits they get from taking those small initial actions, the more likely they'll be to take a bigger action when you ask.

Your Next Steps

- Do the exercise listing your strengths and stories to identify your potential character. Whenever you're creating emails imagine yourself as that character and how they (you) would speak and act.

- Review some of your recent emails (or other writing). Look for how you could make that writing more conversational in tone. And see where you could build in personal stories to make the writing more engaging.

- List the different small actions you could ask your subscribers to take and select ones that fit well with the style of emails you're thinking of sending.

- Review your emails to make sure they include the elements of AIDA. Do they grab your reader's attention? Do they build interest and desire? Is there a clear call to action?

5 BUY ME: TURNING ENGAGED SUBSCRIBERS INTO PAYING CLIENTS

In the previous chapter we talked about engagement and action. Writing the sort of emails that get your subscribers to reply, to click links, to complete surveys. The ultimate action, of course, is for them to buy your product or service (or contribute to your cause or whatever your primary goal is with your emails).

Getting Subscribers Ready to Buy

Exactly how you get your subscribers to buy from you (or do whatever other primary goal you have – but let's assume it's buying to make this easier to explain) is somewhat dependent on the size of commitment you're asking them to make by hiring you or purchasing one of your products. The higher the cost, the bigger the risk, the greater the impact, then the more "persuasion" it's going to take.

It's often said that clients will buy "in their own time". And while that's true to a large degree, it's also true that what you send them in your emails can influence how long it takes.

You see, it's not actually *time* that's the determining factor. There isn't some magic internal clock that ticks over into buy mode at a certain point in time. Whether your subscribers are ready to buy is driven by whether they see (rationally and emotionally) that this is something they want to do, and that you've built up enough trust and credibility that they'll be comfortable doing it with you.

In other words you've got to have addressed the "know and feel" factors we identified when we developed the customer insight map for our ideal client persona in chapter 1. Rather than passively waiting and hoping that the passing of time will get a prospect ready to buy, you can explicitly address the know and feel factors in your emails and accelerate their progress.

Of course, you can't force them to be ready to buy. But you can give them all the information and interaction they need to be ready.

In the last chapter we looked at creating emails based on the goals, aspirations, problems and challenges of your ideal clients. Doing that will motivate them to open and read them. And making them an entertaining read will keep them interested. But to get them ready to buy you need to weave in the know and feel factors that will build the right sort of credibility and trust.

The easiest way to do this is to base the *topics* of your emails on your client's goals, aspirations, problems and challenges, and then *illustrate those topics* using stories, examples and case studies that prove the know and feel factors.

That way subscribers open up the emails because they're focused on topics they're interested in. They get good value from the emails because of the content. But they also, sometimes subconsciously, pick up the know and feel factors too.

So let's say you're a business coach who's recognized that your ideal client's main problem is improving cash flow and they need to know and feel that you've worked with businesses in the retail sector like them. Then instead of just sending them an email with tips on improving cash flow, wrap those tips in a story about a retailer you helped to improve his cash flow. Or an example from your own business back when you used to run a chain of stores. Or write an email discussing the top 3 strategic issues retail business face, and quote some of the key statistics on cash flow and how it can be addressed. Each of these emails will not only provide valuable information, but will get across the impression that you know the retail sector well.

You won't be able to cover one of the know and feel factors in every email you send: it only really works for personal and client stories and case study type emails. But over time you can make sure that within a few weeks of subscribing to your emails your potential clients will have had at least one email related to each know and feel factor.

So your baseline for converting subscribers into buyers is to "warm them up" and get them comfortable hiring you or buying your products through emails that address their specific know and feel factors.

Triggering Action

Your next step is to trigger them into action – to make them an offer that will lead to a sale. This usually takes one of three forms:

- A link in your email to a sales page on your website where they can read about (or watch) what you have to offer, how it will benefit them, and can then buy the product or service online.

- A link to register for a webinar or teleseminar or other one-to-many event where they'll be given more valuable content and at the end of the event be invited to follow up by buying your product or service.

- A link to set up a one-to-one call or meeting with you. This might be a straight sales meeting, or it might be a "strategy session" where you give them some advice (for example, helping to clarify their main goals, identify barriers to achieving them, then agreeing an outline plan for them) and then discuss working together.

You can also, of course, combine the approaches. For example, your email might lead to a webinar where at the end attendees are invited to apply for a strategy session with you.

Usually, a simple sales page is used for lower cost and easier to understand products (typically costing up to a few hundred dollars or pounds, though this can vary by industry). A one-to-one call is usually the best route for more complex, costly services where the potential buyer will need to feel comfortable with you personally and the high price of the service (usually multiple thousand dollars or pounds) justifies your investment of time one-to-one. Webinars typically fall somewhere in the middle – medium priced products and services, or to qualify prospects for a one-to-one call.

What form should your call to actions take?

Here's something that's almost never properly understood: the way you make your call to action is highly dependent on the frequency of your emails.

The reason is that, as we've seen, before someone will take a step like clicking on a link to make a purchase or apply for a one-to-one call, they need to be motivated to do so. And the bigger the step, the more motivation they'll need.

If you're only emailing your subscribers very infrequently, say once a month, then you'll need to put all the reasons they should click that link (and go on to buy your product, register for your webinar or apply for a one-to-one session) into one email.

On the other hand if you're emailing frequently: daily or a few times a week; you can split the "sell" over multiple emails. The first email can focus on one of the benefits of the product; the next can focus on another. The third can deal with a common objection, etc.

This is one of the reasons why I believe that frequent emails are more effective. Having to put a ton of copy into an email to sell the action you'd like them to take makes the email feel more like a sales pitch. It changes the tone away from friendly advisor into salesman.

When your friends and trusted colleagues recommend something to you they typically do it briefly by saying something like "hey, you really should check out the new iWidget app. It really saves you time booking meetings and I think it would work well for you". They don't go on and on and list the 31 reasons why you should follow their recommendation.

An email that's dominated by a big list of benefits you'll get from a product or reasons you should join a webinar feels impersonal and like you're trying to sell to them. A series of emails that have something useful or fun in them and then a few lines on the product or webinar feels like a friend is recommending something.

Which leads us to our next topic…

Can You Sell in Every Email?

Newcomers to email marketing are often told that you shouldn't try to sell in every email, that you should build a relationship first. Or that you should alternate between a series of content emails followed by a pitch email. The idea being that by giving a few emails of useful content first you've earned the right to pitch something.

The problem with this idea is firstly that you never know when people are ready to buy. In fact, when people first subscribe to your emails there's often a good proportion who are ready to take action and buy now – that's why they subscribed. Not giving them the opportunity to buy denies them (and you) something that could help them.

And secondly, a pitch email still feels like a pitch email even if it follows a bunch of content rich ones. People don't like to be pitched to at any time. They don't give you a free pass just because your previous emails have been useful.

The key isn't *when* you sell in your emails or *how frequently*, it's *how you do it*.

As copywriter Daniel Levis says, "of course, if your emails are just blatant pitches you'll annoy people. But effective selling isn't about pitching; *it's about seducing them in your emails*. If people love reading your sales emails then you can sell to them as often as you want".

Now, of course, as a professional copywriter, Daniel has the skills to write seductively that many of us would struggle to match. But it's the mind-set that's important here.

Instead of seeing the sales part or call to action of your emails as some terrible imposition you have to sneak in or "earn the right" to deliver, find ways of making them fit into your emails so that they're seen as part of the value or even entertainment you're delivering.

For example, using the cash flow tips email we mentioned above, by the end of it some of the retail business owners should be thinking, "these are incredibly helpful tips" and "I really ought to do something about cash flow in my business". And maybe "how do I put them into practice?" or "I wish I could get more of this advice".

So to create a call to action that doesn't grate, put yourself in the shoes of your ideal client having just read the email so far and try to figure out what they're likely to be thinking and what questions they're asking. Then write the sales part of the email as the logical next step or answer to that question that leads them in the direction of what you'd like them to do.

If the business coach in our example wanted to get subscribers to contact him for a one-to-one strategy session to discuss working together he could close the email by saying something along the lines of "If you'd like to get the same level of cash flow injection in your business then just hit reply and we'll set up a no-obligation 'cash flow booster' session where we'll review the five most effective tactics for improving cash flow quickly and how you can apply them in your business".

Not every subscriber is going to immediately hit reply to set up a strategy session. In fact the vast majority won't. But every email you send with a call to action linked logically to the content of the email will result in some subscribers taking action and almost none of your subscribers feeling sold to or pitched at.

If you link your call to action to the content of your email so that it's viewed as a natural next step based on what your subscriber is likely to be thinking at that time, then you absolutely can sell in every email. Now you may not want to. You might well have other objectives for specific emails like getting feedback, beginning a discussion, building anticipation for the next email, or just giving out useful information. But there's no reason why you can't sell in every email.

And if you're emailing frequently as I recommend, you don't need to have a perfect call to action in every email, you have plenty more chances in future emails.

Sometimes, for example, I'll simply mention a product in passing and link to it. So I might have a line that says something like "One of the areas we focus on the most in <u>Momentum Club</u> is lead generation..." and then go on to give a tip on lead generation. There's a link to the sales page for Momentum Club, but no overt promotion. If people read the email and want to get more training on lead generation, they'll take the hint and click the link.

Or sometimes I'll just add a simple PS to an email:

"If you found this lead generation tip useful you'll find dozens more in-depth tutorials in Momentum Club. <u>Click here</u> for details".

These links aren't as strong or as likely to get someone to click as building the call to action more naturally into the email as a logical progression from the content. But they work and they're easy to do. One of the big secrets of effective email marketing is that "little and often" almost always beats "big and infrequent". Not the least because you'll actually do little and often whereas you'll put off big in order to try to make it perfect.

Hard Teaching vs. Soft Teaching

Some expert email marketers advocate against "hard teaching". In other words they recommend not giving out too much detailed information in your emails. Their logic is that if you give too much valuable information away, your subscribers will cease to value it (what we get for free we don't value much) and they'll have no need to buy from you if they can get it all for free in your emails.

There's some truth in this viewpoint, but I've found it's very dependent on your situation. If what you sell is primarily information: online courses and e-books; then yes, it is possible to give away so much information in your emails that people have no need to buy your products.

But if, like most people, the primary thing you're selling is a physical product or your services (if you're a consultant or lawyer for example), then the information you give away for free is never going to replace what your clients will get from working with you personally. Where "hard teaching" can hurt in this case is less about people not needing your services. It's more that you can overwhelm them with too much information that they can't take in. Or that because you're focused so much on teaching you forget to entertain. Your emails become more like reading an encyclopaedia than tuning in to your favourite TV show and eventually your subscribers just get bored.

Many successful email marketers do educate and "hard teach" in their emails. But they make sure that their emails are also entertaining, and that they include all the other elements necessary to build relationships, build credibility and secure sales.

Using Email Campaigns

As we've hinted at already, you can magnify the impact of your emails by linking them together in campaigns. This simply means putting together a logical sequence of emails that all work together to achieve a specific outcome – rather than each email being written and standing independently.

A typical campaign can last one to four weeks and will focus on one particular goal. For example the purchase of a specific product or securing a one-to-one call. In this way, if you have multiple products and services in your portfolio (or other outcomes you want to achieve) then rather than trying to sell them all at once, or on haphazardly focusing on one then another, you pick one and focus on it with multiple emails over the period.

To develop a campaign you refine your customer insight map

to be based on just the elements related to the specific product, service or other outcome you're aiming for in the campaign, then create a series of emails which address the relevant know and feel factors and have a consistent call to action focused on the outcome.

You can then tie your emails together and build anticipation between them. In one email you can mention something and say you'll be expanding on it in the next email, for example, increasing the chance that the next email will get opened. Or you can number the emails in series (1 of 7, 2 of 7 etc.) again increasing the chances that your subscriber will open up future emails because they want to get the whole series.

Daniel Levis is the master of these sorts of campaigns for selling specific products. He'll typically craft a set of emails like a series of episodes for a TV show with an overarching theme, consistent characters throughout the emails, and plot links and continuations between emails. He'll usually send out those emails at least daily for a two-week period during the campaign before "resting" and moving on to the next campaign.

Using campaigns like this can multiply the impact of individual emails. Rather than having independent emails each asking your subscriber to do something different every time, by focusing the whole series on a single desired outcome it means that when they read each email it triggers memories of the related points you made in earlier emails, all supporting them taking the same action.

Using Email Campaigns to Drive Webinar Registrations

One of the most effective methods for getting large numbers of sales of medium priced products is to use webinars. In a sales webinar the presenter will share useful hints and tips, build a personal bond with listeners, and then present the product or service as the logical next step for those wanting to get more, better, or faster results in the areas they've been talking about.

In order for webinars to be effective you need to get your subscribers to register for the webinar <u>and</u> to show up (sales are much lower when people just watch a replay afterwards. There's something about the live event and presentation that gives people the confidence to buy).

The more invitations you send, the more registrations you'll get. But you can't simply send the same invitation again and again, or you'll annoy your subscribers. So instead, use a short campaign.

I typically send my first invitation about a week in advance of the webinar. Exact timings will vary for your specific niche, but emailing too early generally results in people ignoring your message.

My first email will be a straight invitation where I announce the webinar, list what we'll be covering, when it's scheduled for, how attendees will benefit from it, and give the registration link.

I'll then do two to three further invitations. These invitations tend to be more story based emails, or emails with tips about the topic I'll be covering on the webinar as a preview and teaser of the content they'd get if they attended. Emails I've used in the past have included:

- A review of current business trends highlighting why the

topic of the webinar is so important.

- A story from my own experience or one of my clients showing the benefits you can get from mastering the topic.

- One or two useful tips that are shortened versions of what they'll experience on the webinar.

- An example showing how the topic is relevant even if they think it might not be (e.g. how email marketing can work when your clients are large corporates, not just small businesses).

The trick with these follow-up invitations is to provide something interesting in the email so that the reader feels they've got value from it even if they don't register for the webinar.

I'll also do a short, last minute invite a few hours before the webinar to catch people who didn't think they'd be available but now find they have some free time. That email is usually very short with just the login details for the webinar.

Depending on what webinar system you use, you should configure the registration process to also subscribe the people who register for a series of "warm up" emails designed to increase attendance at the webinar. These can include:

- A reminder of the benefits of the webinar and reasons to attend live.

- Asking registrants questions which you then answer live on the webinar.

- Giving registrants an exercise to do that they'll use on the webinar.

- Giving registrants a set of notes for the webinar that further tease and preview the content.

Then finally, after the webinar you'll send a series of follow-up emails reinforcing the call to action made in the webinar. These can include:

- An email thanking them for attending.

- An email with a link to a replay of the webinar.

- Emails with further tips expanding on some of the content.

- Emails revealing new bonuses you've added to the product.

- An "offer closing" email if your call to action was time bound.

In each email you have the content of the email followed by a summary of the call to action (buying a product, scheduling a call etc.) made in the webinar.

Using Email to Get One-To-One Calls

For many businesses, a sale is almost always preceded by a one-to-one call or meeting. For service businesses like coaching and consulting, accounting or law, your potential client will want to speak to you directly before they'll be comfortable hiring you. And for large purchases, the sheer size of the purchase, the complexity of the decision-making, and the questions a customer will want to ask before buying make direct contact a must.

In these cases, your goal for email marketing should be to secure that one-to-one call or meeting. That could be a simple sales call where a potential client speaks to you about working together. Or it could be strategy session or free consultation you offer where you spend 20-40 minutes in a structured discussion with a potential client reviewing their goals and challenges and helping them plan how they'll address them before discussing the option of working together.

At the simplest level, you can make your call to action at the end of your emails an offer of a strategy session or recommendation to call you if they'd like to discuss working with you to achieve similar results to those you mention in the email (if, for example, you've just done a case study email).

You can ask people to contact you by phone, or by replying to the email. But as your list of subscribers gets bigger and the number of meeting requests grows, you may want to send people to an "application form" on the web where they supply details about themselves and/or their business which would enable you to qualify if they'd be a good fit for working with you.

It can also make sense to combine this approach with some of the engagement strategies discussed in the previous chapter to give a two-stage approach to offering a strategy session.

If you ask a question in one of your emails like "tell me your biggest problem with X?" then those subscribers that send you details of their problem have essentially self-identified as having an issue big enough and important enough to them that they're willing to ask for help with it. They've also shown that they trust you at least enough to share their problem with.

So if you email them back some initial ideas and then offer a strategy session or call, you've done two things:

1. You've focused your offer on only those people who have a problem you can help with and for whom it's an important issue.

2. You've already given some help and ideas to them through your initial response, which makes it more likely they'll agree to a call with you.

A final strategy for one-to-one sessions is to charge for them. If you have a steady stream of people requesting sessions then the simplest solution to ensure you're focusing on people who are serious about working with you and will be motivated to follow through is to test that commitment by charging.

The usual approach is to charge a fee for the session but to make it risk-free by offering a complete refund if the session doesn't achieve what the potential client is looking for. And if you do decide to work together further, the fee for the session is often offset against the fees for that larger piece of work.

The overarching strategy here is that for higher value products and services you should see your email marketing not as a way of selling without human involvement (that just won't happen for large sales), but as a way of efficiently "teeing up" the right level of involvement with the right people. Your email marketing gets potential clients ready to speak to you, it gets them as ready as is possible to buy, and it gets the right people talking to you so you can focus your scarce one-to-one time in the areas most likely to result in a sale.

Summary

The key steps to getting subscribers to buy are:

- Engaging with them and getting them to take small actions in your earlier emails.

- Demonstrating the "know and feel factors" that they need to see to feel comfortable buying.

- Positioning your sales offer as the logical next step for them based on what they've heard from you so far.

- Emailing frequently and including a call to action in each email so that you don't have to make a huge sales pitch in one email. Seduce them into buying rather than pitching at them.

- Developing focused campaigns that consistently promote one single call to action or sale rather than jumping from offer to offer with each email.

- Using webinars and one-to-one calls as the next step for higher value products and services.

Your Next Steps

- Pick a specific product or service that you want to promote in your emails. Go back to your customer insight map and identify from that map which "know and feel" factors specifically relate to this product or service.

- Review some of your existing or planned emails to see how you can build in the "know and feel" factors as stories, examples or case studies.

- Decide on whether you can promote the product or service directly, or whether you need to promote a webinar or one-to-one call which then sells the product or service.

- Think of how you can embed calls to action to promote the product or service into some of your existing or planned emails. Which emails address problems or challenges that the product or service then goes on to cover in more depth?

- Review how you could tie the relevant emails together in a short campaign. How can they be sequenced to form a coherent story?

6 AUTOPILOT MARKETING: USING "AUTORESPONDERS" TO AUTOMATE YOUR EMAIL MARKETING

Much of email marketing is done as "broadcasts". You create an email and send it out to all (or a subset of) your subscribers at the same time.

However, it's also possible to pre-program your emails and have them sent out in sequence, usually based on when your subscriber signed up. Using this "autoresponder" method means that rather than everyone getting the same email at the same time as they would with a broadcast, everyone gets Email 1 when they sign up, Email 2 a day later, Email 3 a few days later, etc. (depending on how you set up the timing of the sequence).

The Advantages of Email Autoresponders

Using autoresponders has three big advantages over manually broadcasting. Firstly it means that everyone will get your very best emails. With broadcasts, a new subscriber won't get to see that brilliant email you sent out three weeks ago because they weren't on your list at the time.

Secondly, it means you can tailor your emails based on where an individual subscriber is likely to be in their relationship with you and what they've seen from you already. With a broadcast, the same email goes to people who've been subscribers for ten years or ten days. With an autoresponder sequence you can schedule emails covering the basics to be sent early in the sequence, and more advanced material or material that assumes the reader knows you quite well later in the sequence. You can also send emails that assume prior knowledge of earlier emails in the sequence, or that look forward to later emails. Whereas with broadcasts you run the risk of referring to an email from before the reader subscribed.

Finally, autoresponders are "set and forget". Create a long enough sequence and you can have emails going out to subscribers triggering actions and purchases for months or even years after they sign up without you needing to create any new material.

Broadcasts, however, have the advantage of allowing you to tap in to breaking news or deal with live events. If all your emails have been pre-programmed, it's difficult to announce a new product or invite people to a webinar, or to comment on how yesterday's surprise sporting hero makes a great point about your product.

Autoresponder sequences are usually triggered by a subscriber signing up to your emails. But in more advanced systems they can be triggered by actions like clicking a link, visiting a web page or buying a product. In the latter case, a great use of an autoresponder is to send a sequence of customer care emails. Congratulating the buyer, sending them information on how best to use their product, reassuring them of your availability for support, etc. A customer care sequence like this can significantly reduce post-purchase anxiety and refunds.

Options for Autoresponders

When subscribers first sign up for your emails you have a number of choices for how you apply autoresponders:

- You could just start sending them broadcasts from day one

without using autoresponders at all.

- You could send new subscribers a short "start-up" sequence of emails with a specific end goal in mind. Right now, people who sign up for my emails at ianbrodie.com get sent my "5 Simple Marketing Tweaks That Will Get You More Clients" report, followed by a series of five short videos giving them an insight into my Client Flow process for winning clients, followed by an invitation to a webinar. My goals for this are firstly to expose them to some of my best material early on to quickly build credibility and trust. Secondly to get them used to receiving frequent emails from me and to getting value from those emails. And finally to showcase the sort of material they'd get access to if they joined my paid membership program and to encourage them to join.

- You could put them on a long-term "set and forget" autoresponder that will manage all emails to them. MindValley, for example, typically tries to create autoresponders at least 100 days long for each of their core products. During that time they'll have pre-programmed emails that cover the type of issues the product addresses, give useful advice, cover off all the know and feel factors at least once, answer frequently asked questions, share inspiring stories and encourage interaction.

- You could chain together shorter sequences focused on different products, services or other desired outcomes. So a business coach might focus the first few weeks on emails related to her entry-level online training course, but then move on to a sequence where the call to action is for a one-to-one call to discuss working together personally.

You can also mix sequences with broadcasts to try to get the best of both worlds. For my emails, once subscribers finish the initial start-up sequence with videos and the webinar invite, they go onto a sequence where they get some of my best content emails every Sunday morning. In between those pre-programmed emails I'll send broadcast emails 2-3 times during the week itself. This allows me to send live webinar invites and react to events or feedback in real-time during the week while still ensuring that subscribers are getting some of my all-time best emails at the weekend.

Planning an Autoresponder Sequence

Planning an autoresponder sequence is a bit like plotting a movie or book. You usually start off with an overall theme or vision for the plot, along with ideas for some of the key scenes in the movie or chapters and passages in the book. You then "storyboard" the movie by brainstorming new ideas and sequencing how all the scenes fit together. It's an iterative process. And in the case of email autoresponders, one you can keep improving over time.

It's essentially an expanded version of designing the short campaigns we covered in the previous chapter. Pick a single goal you want your sequence of emails to achieve: an action you'd like your subscribers to take like buying a specific product or setting up a one-to-one call.

Then review your Customer Insight Map for your ideal client and pull out all the goals, aspirations, problems and challenges they have related to that area, along with the relevant know and feel factors.

The goals, aspirations, problems and challenges will give you ideas for topics for your emails in the sequence; the know and feel factors will be the things you need to illustrate in your stories, examples, case studies and anecdotes that you use to cover each topic.

Do an audit of all the resources you already have available to you. What blog posts, videos, audio, infographics, previous emails or other content resources have you already created that you can link to or cover in the email itself that would be useful for your subscribers and cover one of the topics you have listed? What stories and case studies have you already prepared that you could rework into email format?

By now you should have a decent list of potential topics to go into your sequence. And for many of the topics you should have a variety of potential resources and ideas lined up for the content. For your first sequence, don't overcomplicate things: aim for about 6-12 emails initially, you can always add more later.

To work out the order of the sequence I like to write each topic on a post-it note so I can then move them around and re-sequence them until the sequence of topics make sense. Typically you'll want to make sure that your first emails focus on the most immediate and pressing problems or goals your subscribers have as those will be the areas they've got the biggest sense of urgency in reading about. And you'll also want to make sure that any hints, tips and insights you share early on are your simplest, most practical ones. Later on you can share some of the more complex ideas and build on some of the foundations you lay down early on.

You might also want to follow MindValley's lead and try to balance out the types of emails you're sending to get a mix of content emails, sales focused emails, engagement emails and inspirational emails. And if you keep your emails relatively short early on, you'll find your subscribers get into the habit of seeing them as an easy read. Later on, once the association between your emails and valuable information entertainingly written has been established you can afford to write much longer emails if needed.

After you've got the basic sequence planned out, you can begin to work on the content of each email. Start by defining the call to action you're going to use in each email, then create the appropriate email subject line and content.

Here's an outline of a short email sequence that a business coach might use for new subscribers. You can get a copy of each email in the sequence in the bonus section of the Email Persuasion website at www.emailpersuasion.com/bonuses.

Overall Goal: Encourage new subscribers to sign up for a one-to-one "business breakthrough" call.

Timing: Starts immediately after subscribers sign up for free copy of "Breakthrough to Growth" report. Emails sent every two to three days.

Email 1: Did you get your "Breakthrough to Growth" report?

Goals:

- Make sure new subscribers got the report and they're reading it.
- Establish friendly conversational tone and encourage interaction.
- Get people who are ready for one-to-one call already to book one.

Call to Action: Apply for a free "business breakthrough" call

Email 2: What's your biggest business challenge right now?

Goals:

- Get subscribers used to taking action
- Identify subscribers who have significant challenges and are ready to discuss them

Call to Action: Email me to tell me about your biggest challenge. I'll send you my best ideas to help by return.

Email 3: Hope is not a strategy

Goals:

- Establish importance of taking action rather than just passively consuming information

Call to Action: If you'd like to take immediate action to accelerate the growth of your business then email me to set up a free "business breakthrough" call.

Email 4: My cash flow struggle

Goals:

- Establish empathy, that I've been in the same position as them
- To show them I know how to fix cash flow problems quickly

Call to Action: If you're facing similar problems with cash flow I can probably help. Fast. Just hit reply and we'll set up a quick discussion to give you some ideas and practical next steps.

Email 5: The 7 growth barriers all small businesses hit

Goals:

- Demonstrate knowledge of key areas needed to grow a small business and ability to simplify and make sense of problems
- Showcase case studies of successful client work across likely range of client industries (services, retail, financial, manufacturing)

Call to Action: For a review of your business and how you can break through these growth barriers, call me to set up a free "business breakthrough" session.

Email 6: Can you help me?

Goals:

- Encourage interaction and gather information on key topics of interest to subscribers by asking for help with survey

Call to Action: Click this link to take the survey.

Summary

You can enhance the effectiveness of your emails and put your marketing on autopilot by creating autoresponders: linked sequences of emails delivered sequentially after a subscriber signs up or performs some other action.

Autoresponders can be "storyboarded" rather like a film with each email building to achieve an overall goal. Autoresponders can be used particularly well when new subscribers join your list, or for new buyers of your products.

Your Next Steps

- Decide on where you'd like to use autoresponders in your email marketing. At minimum, consider an autoresponder sequence of your best emails for when new subscribers join your list.

- Write down an overall goal for your autoresponder sequence then from your customer insight map pick out all the related problems, challenges, goals and aspirations and "know and feel" factors.

- List all the available resources you have that you could bring together in the sequence (e.g. blog posts, videos, previous emails).

- Write down the main topics you think would make up your story based on the problems, challenges, goals and aspirations you've identified and try to place them into a logical or interesting sequence that flows as a story.

- Flesh out each email in the sequence by adding a call to action, the subject line of the email, and the contents of each email.

7 TAILORING YOUR EMAILS: USING LIST SEGMENTATION TO GET THE RIGHT MESSAGE TO THE RIGHT SUBSCRIBER

One of the biggest challenges of email marketing, especially when you build up a relatively large subscriber base, is finding the right balance in your emails to get the best results. This applies to the frequency of emails, the topics you cover, how much you promote vs. share content, etc.

The underlying issue is variety in your subscriber base. In any large group of subscribers you'll find some for whom you're not emailing often enough, and some for whom you're emailing too often. There'll be some who want more emails on a specific topic, and others who want fewer. There'll be some who are ready to buy and want all the details you can give them about a particular product or service, and others who aren't interested in that specific product for whom that'll be a huge turnoff (even though they may be great prospects for other products and services in future).

The problem is that if you try to hit a middle ground, you'll please no one. Your sales emails, for example, will be too long and too numerous for the people who aren't interested in the product. But they won't be frequent enough or contain enough details to fully persuade the people who are interested.

One advanced approach to email marketing that resolves this issue is **list segmentation**. When you segment a list you split out subscribers who match certain characteristics and send them different or additional emails to those who don't match the characteristics.

Emailing Based on Interest

If you knew exactly who was interested in a particular product or service, you could send your sales emails only to them and not to the people who weren't interested. Depending on the capabilities of your email system, this can be done in a variety of ways:

1. You can "tag" subscribers based on which previous emails they've opened and clicked on, or which web pages they've visited. In that way you can identify who has shown a prior interest in a topic.

2. You can email all your subscribers about a specific topic and offer further information for those interested, then restrict the follow up to those that take up the offer (either by clicking a link, visiting a web page or opting-in to a new list). In this way you identify who is interested in a topic right now.

So let's say you're a business coach who's created a training product related to Linkedin. Following the first method what you'd do is in previous emails, every time you link from an email to an article on Linkedin or social media on your website you tag the subscribers who go off to read it. When you launch your product you send more emails about it to the tagged subscribers, knowing that they've shown an interest in Linkedin related material in the past so extra emails are more likely to result in increased sales rather than increased unsubscribes.

In the second case what you'd do is create a new free resource (a PDF download, video, webinar or just an article on your site about using Linkedin) and send an email offering this resource to all your subscribers. Those subscribers who take up the offer (by opting in to a new list or clicking a link for example) would get put on a short email sequence that then sends them the information you promised and follows up with information about your Linkedin product (probably along with more useful Linkedin tips).

In both cases, because you know which subscribers are more interested in Linkedin you can send more relevant material to them and less to the people who don't indicate an interest. The result: both groups are happier and you get more sales and fewer unsubscribes.

Emailing Based on Engagement Level

One useful approach which uses list segmentation is to tailor the emails you send to subscribers based on their level of engagement.

A simple example of this is with your start-up sequence that subscribers get when first joining your email list. If you plan to send links to four or five short videos to your new subscribers then rather than just sending them a string of emails on a fixed schedule irrespective of whether they're actually watching the videos or not, schedule your emails so that you only send out the next email in sequence after your subscriber has watched the previous video. For subscribers who haven't watched the videos send them a couple of reminders before moving them on to the next video.

That way your most engaged subscribers move on quickly through the videos. But those who haven't had time to watch them don't get overwhelmed when the next video in sequence comes through before they've had a chance to watch the first one.

Similarly, you can also use list segmentation to try to re-engage with subscribers who've stopped opening and reading your emails. Most email systems will allow you to identify which subscribers haven't opened or clicked your emails for some time (although the open rate statistics are often far from accurate). You can then add them to an autoresponder sequence that tries to tempt them back into becoming an active subscriber, or removes them from your list if they don't. Either way is a win for you as you either get a re-engaged subscriber, or an inactive subscriber removed from your list so your deliverability will improve.

List Segmentation to Increase Response

You can also use list segmentation to increase your response in a number of ways. For example:

- Emailing subscribers based in a specific geographic area when you're running a live event.

- Making a special offer to subscribers who visited a sales or checkout page but didn't complete the transaction.

- Emailing offers of related products to subscribers based on previous purchases, or on age, sex or other demographics.

- Emailing a one-to-one session offer to subscribers who've recently started browsing your site more often or have been opening and clicking more emails.

Each of these tactics gets your offers and other emails into the inboxes of the subscribers most likely to appreciate them, and doesn't risk over emailing or emailing irrelevant offers to people less likely to appreciate them.

These approaches rely on having additional data available about your subscribers. Some of it can be gathered behaviourally (collecting data on link clicks or website pages visited if your system is capable of doing this). Other demographic data requires your subscribers to provide that information.

As we saw in chapter 2 on getting email subscribers, the more data you ask people to provide, the less likely they are to opt-in, so you're best off gathering data in stages. Just go for name and email address initially, but once you have this you can ask for more later.

So you could gather some basic demographic data as part of a survey you invite them to take. Or you could offer further free resources (PDFs, videos, etc.) and on the download form you can prefill the data you already have (name and email) and ask for more. Hubspot does this with many of their more in-depth free reports, asking for company name, website and job title after you've already opted in with just your name and email address.

If you're confident in the value of knowing the extra information you can also invest to get it. If you've written a book or if you record an audio on CD you can offer to send a free copy to subscribers who will need to provide you with their name and address for you to send it to. You can then use that geographic information to send more relevant emails, like notification of a local event.

Summary

List segmentation is a technique for splitting your subscribers into groups and emailing different things to each group. By doing this you can ensure you're sending the right messages with the right frequency to each group. This is particularly valuable when you're promoting products and services so that the people who are genuinely interested get enough information to make a decision and the people who aren't interested don't get bombarded with sales messages.

Your Next Steps

- First decide if you're ready for list segmentation. If you're in the early stages of building your list and learning how to email effectively then save it for later once you've mastered the basics.

- Check your email system to see what its list segmentation capabilities are. Check for the ability to tag contacts and to trigger emails and sequences based on tags and actions (like clicking links or visiting web pages) or whether subscribers will need to re-opt-in to get onto additional sequences.

- Decide what will trigger your additional sequence of emails. Will it be based on previous subscriber behaviour (if so you'll need to start tracking it)? Or will it be based on a subscriber requesting more information about a specific topic?

- Sketch out the different paths subscribers will go down and the emails they should receive. Make sure you're sending the right number and content of emails to both.

8 PERSUADING WITH EMAIL: LEARNING THE SCIENCE OF INFLUENCE

If we're going to be using email to persuade potential clients to work with us or buy our products or services, we need to understand how persuasion works. What is it that gets people to buy or take action? And then we need to build those factors into our email marketing.

And let's be clear here: by "persuasion" I don't mean manipulation or trickery.

The Oxford English Dictionary defines persuasion as "to induce (someone) to do something through reasoning or argument". In other words you give them the information and logic needed to allow them to make a decision. For me, that's the best definition for the sort of persuasion we use in email marketing.

We're not emailing our subscribers (just) because we like them. We're not emailing them because we want to be their best friend. We're emailing them because we want them to (eventually) buy from us, or join our cause or take some action we'd like them to take. But we're doing it in a way that's ethical. We're giving them information to allow them to make a decision. Whether they then decide to buy, join or take action is up to them.

There are three major factors we need to master in order to persuade: our target client's motivation, the principles of clear and effective communication, and the tools of persuasion.

Motivation

The first key factor is our **target client's motivation**. What is it that they want to achieve?

Legendary copywriter Eugene Schwartz said in his book *Breakthrough Advertising*[13], "Let's get to the heart of the matter. The power, the force, the overwhelming urge to own that makes advertising work, comes from the market itself, and not from the copy.

Copy cannot create desire for a product. It can only take the hopes, dreams, fears and desires that already exists in the hearts of millions of people, and focus those already existing desires onto a particular product."

In other words, by far the most effective way to persuade someone to do something is not to try to convince them that they want to do that thing. It's to understand *what they already want*, and then *show them how they can get it* by doing that something.

Want someone to buy your new leadership training course? If they already want to go on a leadership training course that's great. But chances are they don't. What they probably want is a better job, more money, a fulfilling career, a sense of mastery and achievement. Show them how your leadership training course will give them that and you're far more likely to get their interest.

As marketing coach Dov Gordon explains, "buyers buy simply based on whether you can *get rid of a problem they have and don't want*, or *enable them to get something they want but don't have*".

It's rare that what you're selling or asking them to do will be the thing they want directly. It's much more likely that your thing

---

[13] Eugene Schwartz, *Breakthrough Advertising*, Prentice-Hall, 1966.

will be something that helps them get it. And it's also highly likely that initially they won't see the connection. By uncovering what it is that your specific ideal clients want to achieve and then connecting the dots for them to your product or service, you'll unleash their motivation to buy.

That's why we placed so much emphasis in chapter 1 on building deep understanding of your ideal clients. That level of understanding allows you to position your offers and calls to action in the context of what your ideal clients already want. That's the foundation of persuasive email.

Clear and Effective Communication

Once you have that foundation, you can then harness the second factor: **clear and effective communication.**

Having a perfect understanding of your ideal client's motivation and knowing how your products and services can help is of little use if you fail to communicate that to them. Email, after all, is a communication channel.

Effective email communication means:

- Being laser-focused on what you want to achieve with your email – overall and for each individual email - and translating those into simple, clear messages.

- Communicating those messages clearly, in language that connects with your ideal client.

- Grabbing the attention of your reader and holding it until you've got your message across.

That's why in chapter 3 we looked in-depth at effective email subject lines and in chapters 4 and 5 we reviewed techniques for clear and engaging communication.

Tools of Persuasion

Once you've understood your ideal client's primary motivation and you can communicate with them clearly and effectively, the third and final factor comes into play: **the tools of persuasion**. Techniques and methods for influencing based on sound psychological principles and experience.

For centuries, salespeople, politicians and leaders of all types have used these tools, often instinctively. Yet it's only fairly recently that the skills and techniques of influence have been studied and tested scientifically.

Perhaps the best exposition of these persuasion tools comes from Dr Robert Cialdini in his book *Influence: The Psychology of Persuasion*[14].

Cialdini outlined six "weapons of persuasion" that will amplify the success of your attempts to persuade people to your point of view. Of course, without a deep understanding of what it is your clients really want, and without being able to communicate effectively, these weapons are of little use. But once you have those foundations in place they can significantly enhance your results.

You may have seen these principles before, but let's look at how we can use them specifically in email marketing.

Principle 1: Reciprocity. Our tendency as humans to return favours, pay back debts and treat others as we've been treated ourselves.

In a classic experiment to illustrate this[15], researchers found

---

[14] Dr Robert Cialdini, *Influence: The Psychology of Persuasion*, Collins, 1984.

[15] Strohmetz, Rind, Fisher and Lynn, *Sweetening the Till: The Use of Candy to Increase Restaurant Tipping*, Journal of Applied Social Psychology, Feb 2002.

that when restaurant waiters gave a mint with the check to customers, their tips increased by 3 to 4%. If they gave two mints, the tips went up 9 to 12%. Reciprocity at work.

But the final stage of the experiment was even more revealing. This time the waiter was told to leave the check on the table with one mint, then to step away, hesitate, turn back around and give the table a second mint with words along the lines of "You know, for being so special, here is an extra mint for each of you."

The result of this simple change: tips increased by 2%.

In terms of email marketing, it's pretty well established that an effective method to get people to sign up for your emails is to offer them something of value in return: a free report or video for example. That's not reciprocity; it's simply an incentive to subscribe.

But what you can do to establish reciprocity is the equivalent of the "extra mint" strategy. After people have subscribed, give them an unexpected bonus. An extra free report, an audio version for their iPod or a hard copy through the post. Doing something unexpected, personal and nice then primes your new subscriber to do you a favour in return. Perhaps to tweet a link to your sign up page or give you a short testimonial about the quality of the report.

You can repeat this technique in later emails. Every now and then do something unexpected and special for your subscribers. Give them free access to a small product you normally charge for. Invite them to a subscribers-only event or webinar. Don't do this too frequently or it will become expected. You need to take your subscribers by surprise to get the "free mint" effect.

Principle 2: Social Proof. We're more likely to do something if we see others who are like us do it, too.

Businesses have long used testimonials and quotes from happy customers (with permission, of course) not just to provide factual proof that their products and services work, but to provide social proof that they're popular with others "just like you".

From an email marketing perspective, you can use social proof to encourage signups for your emails. As we saw earlier, Laura Roeder was able to increase signups by 24% simply by adding the quote "Yours is the only newsletter I actually read" to the top of the subscription form on her home page.

You can also use social proof within your emails. Want to encourage people to buy your product or service? Rather than just telling them about the benefits they'll get from it, show them the benefits some of your other customers have got from it. That combines both the motivation to buy with social proof that others are buying it.

Use stories and examples from your clients to illustrate the main points you want to make in your emails and not only will your subscribers get value from them, they'll remember that others like them have been successful by working with or buying from you.

Principle 3: Commitment and Consistency. Once we commit to something – especially publicly – we like to follow through.

In another classic experiment[16], researchers set up a fake theft on a beach. In one arm of the test, the "victim" left a beach towel and portable radio without saying anything. Four times out of twenty, when the thief attempted to steal them, nearby bystanders stepped in. In the second arm, the "victim" asked a nearby person to watch their stuff. In this case, the thief was challenged 19 times

---

[16] Thomas Moriarty, *Crime, commitment, and the responsive bystander: Two field experiments*, Journal of Personality and Social Psychology, Feb 1975.

out of 20. A small initial commitment led to a bigger but consistent action.

Back in the real world, Chicago restaurateur Gordon Sinclair reduced the number of no-shows on bookings from 30% to 10% by switching the wording his staff used when taking the booking from saying "Please call if you change your plans" to "Will you call us if you change your plans?" and waiting until the caller said yes. This simple commitment made all the difference[17].

How does this work in email marketing? One simple example is to start asking subscribers to begin interacting with you in a small way right from when you start communicating with them. Ask them to reply to a message, like or share a blog post, complete a survey. Taking these small steps to interact early on makes it much more likely they'll be willing to take bigger steps later – like joining you on a webinar, arranging a call with you or buying a product.

You can also offer a low cost product early on in your interactions with a subscriber. It's less of a commitment than a high end product or hiring your services. But by purchasing from you they begin to see themselves as a buyer and they're more likely to buy again in future. Especially if their buying and post-purchase experience is very positive.

Principle 4: Liking. We tend to be more influenced by people we know and like than those we don't. This might be because they're like us, they've complimented us or we just feel they're likeable people.

---

[17] Cited in Robert Cialdini, *The Science of Persuasion*, Scientific American, Feb 2001.

In 2005, researcher Randy Garner mailed out surveys to strangers with a request to return them[18]. Some of the requests were signed with a random name, the others with a name that sounded a bit like the name of the recipient. So if they were writing to me, Ian Brodie, they might have sent it from Ian Bailey. Garner found that for the random names, 30% of recipients returned the survey. For the similar names, 56% did.

When you email potential clients and customers, some of the stories you use to illustrate your points can be based on your own experiences. The more those experiences match up with those of your potential buyers, the more likely it is that they'll feel good about buying from you because you feel like "one of us". Some marketers have found that being fairly outspoken in their emails and expressing strong political, ethical or religious views tends to repel a number of subscribers who don't agree with them, but significantly enhances their appeal to those who share similar views. Those with similar views are then much more likely to buy from them – even if the products and services they sell have no relation to the views being expressed.

Personally, I find that just being a nice guy works for me. Responding to emails and questions people send. Going out of my way to be helpful. It's no surprise that the people who get the most from my products and who take up my offer of personal support are the ones who often go on to buy further products and higher end services from me.

Principle 5: Authority. We tend to obey authority figures and do what they ask.

---

[18] Randy Garner, *What's in a Name? Persuasion Perhaps*, Journal of Applied Consumer Psychology, Volume 15 (2), 2005.

I'm sure you've heard of the Milgram experiments at Yale in the 1970s where volunteers were quite willing to inflict quite severe (or so they thought) electric shocks on others simply because they were asked to by white coat wearing experimenters. Similarly, researchers in Texas[19] found that when they crossed the road illegally wearing a suit and tie, 3.5 times as many people followed their lead as when they were dressed casually.

In email marketing, establishing yourself as a credible authority in your field by regularly sending high value, insightful material is one of the core strategies for building influence. And you can boost this by subtly mentioning any books you've written or awards and achievements you've won.

Principle 6: Scarcity. We want what we can't have.

This is one of the most used (and abused) principles in marketing. Sales, exclusive offers, limited editions; all play to our desire to have something that few others have, or that's only available for a limited time.

It's also possible to apply scarcity to email marketing, but I'd advise caution. Many of the things you'll be promoting via email aren't naturally scarce. There are rarely limits on how many people can access your online training, and there's no reason why that software you're selling suddenly won't be available tomorrow.

There are some things that are genuinely scarce: you only have so much time to do strategy calls every month. If you're running a training course with live webinars and feedback for participants there's a genuine deadline that people will need to sign up by otherwise they'll miss it.

---

[19] Lefkowitz, Blake & Mouton, *Status factors in pedestrian violation of traffic signals*, The Journal of Abnormal and Social Psychology, Volume 51 (3), 1955.

But don't fake scarcity. In fact don't fake any of the persuasion principles. Partly because you may well get found out. But more importantly, because it's wrong.

Use the principles when they genuinely apply rather than to manipulate. Communicate your genuine authority. Tell subscribers when something genuinely is scarce. Use genuine testimonials and feedback for social proof.

Summary

Persuasive emails are based on three core factors: understanding what your ideal clients really want, communicating with them clearly, and using the tools of persuasion to get across the information your subscribers need to make decisions.

Your Next Steps

- Review each of your key emails (e.g. those in autoresponder sequences) to see whether one or more of the tools of persuasion could be used to boost their effectiveness.

9 MEASURING AND TESTING YOUR EMAIL MARKETING

Because it's all done online, email is inherently more measurable than almost any other form of marketing. Unfortunately, it's easy to get buried in the minutiae of open rates and clicks and lose sight of the big picture.

The ultimate measure of your email success is whether or not you achieve the end results you're looking for. For most people that will be sales.

Rather than obsessing about how many people are opening your emails (which can be notoriously inaccurate) or how many people are clicking your links, focus first on the sales you're generating through email. There are many instances where by writing email subject lines that are very focused on specific prospects and specific desires, you can get lower open rates and click-through rates, but higher sales.

Sometimes sales attributable to email are not so easy to measure. If you take orders primarily offline (for example, if you're a consultant and clients seal the deal over the phone and pay by direct bank transfer) then there may not be an obvious link back to how that client was nurtured through email. Make sure that for large offline sales like this you check back in your email system to see whether the client is a subscriber. And always ask them too: they may have subscribed under a different name and email address.

For other businesses, for example retailers doing marketing via multiple channels, a customer purchase is often triggered by interactions across more than one of those channels. They may have received a series of emails over time raising their awareness of the store and its offers, and then heard an ad on radio alerting them to an upcoming sale event. The only way to tell how much of a contribution email is making in these more complex situations is to do a mail/holdout test by not mailing to a specific segment of your subscriber base for a certain amount of time and checking the sales impact across other channels. For more details on measuring the impact of email in these more complex situations, refer to Kevin Hillstrom's excellent e-book: *Hillstrom's Email Marketing Excellence*[20]

Thankfully, most of us don't have to deal with such complex situations. Most of us will have fairly integrated marketing where email is a critical and identifiable component of most sales.

Building a Simple Email Marketing Dashboard

For most businesses, my recommended approach to metrics is to build a dashboard as follows:

1. Start by calculating the total sales attributable to email each month. For most businesses you can take the sum of your online sales, plus the offline sales (like the consulting clients in the example above) where you can confirm email played a key role. Obviously you want this figure to increase month on month – though there will be an inevitable variability when you have large purchases with a long sales cycle.

2. To get more insight into your sales, keep track of your total

---

[20] Kevin Hillstrom, *Hillstrom's Email Marketing Excellence*, Hillstrom, 2012.

number of subscribers, the average sales per subscriber and track the percentage month on month growth in each. Again you want to see both numbers rising. Sales per subscriber tells you how effective your emails are at building credibility and trust and getting subscribers to take action. Subscriber growth tells you how effective you are at bringing new subscribers in to the fold.

3. For more insights, calculate the total number of buyers each month, and the sales per buyer. This tells you whether you are continuing to get more people to buy, or whether sales are growing simply because the same set of buyers is buying more from you. Depending on your strategy, it may be OK to have fewer buyers buying more, or it may be a sign that your sales will dip in future as that group of buyers runs out of things to buy from you.

These top level metrics will give you an insight into the health of your overall email marketing system based on two overarching goals: get more people into the system and get better results from the subscribers already in there. It's focused on sales because ultimately, that's what you're doing email marketing for. If your sales aren't increasing, you can use the metrics to track down whether that's because you're not growing your subscriber base fast enough, you're not turning enough subscribers into buyers, or your buyers aren't buying enough.

You can't always take the numbers at face value, however. If what you sell is "lumpy", a high value product or service with a long sales cycle, then you'll get a lot of variability in sales month on month that you need to take into account. And you'll also need to factor out temporary promotions or new product and service launches. But overall, this dashboard can give you a very quick way of identifying whether you're on track with your email marketing and if not, what the key issues are.

Given enough time, you can also establish an approximation for the lifetime value of a subscriber. This metric is important because combined with knowing your opt-in rate, it tells you how much you can afford to pay in advertising or other fees for traffic to your landing pages and still remain profitable. When MindValley launches a new product they pay for a small amount of online advertising to get enough traffic to their landing pages while they tweak their initial autoresponder sequence until they're confident they can earn at least a few dollars per subscriber. Once they know that, they rapidly scale up the advertising, confident that they can earn a positive return on investment for every click they pay for.

Measuring and Testing Individual Elements of Your System

Measuring the effectiveness of individual elements such as specific emails or opt-in forms is not as easy as it might seem. Sales or clicks or opens on most emails are dependent on earlier emails you've sent. When someone clicks a link in an email to buy something it's often the culmination of the impact of many earlier emails they've read not just that email. And for opt-in forms, although it's easy to measure which form gets a higher opt-in rate, what you really care about is whether the opt-ins from that form lead to higher sales than the other: not necessarily so easy to measure.

So use metrics at an individual email level as a starting point for further testing – rather than as definitive proof that a certain email or form is good or bad.

Start, of course, by looking at sales or whatever your goal is for your email (for example one-to-one sessions being set up). If sales are particularly disappointing from a specific email then check the email open rate and the click-through rate for your call to action.

If the open rate is lower than other emails, the problem may be your subject line. If the open rate isn't unusually low then it may be that the body of your email and the call to action itself isn't compelling.

Again, sales are the ultimate arbiter. It's OK to have low open rates and click-through rates as long as sales are good. But if sales are lower than other comparable emails then it's worth looking at your open and click-through rates.

It's also worth noting that because email opens are measured by email systems embedding a tiny image in the email and tracking whether that image is accessed on their servers or not, you won't get opens registered for any subscribers who have images switched off in their mail system. Because of this, open rates are quite unreliable measures, though they tend to be consistent for the same set of subscribers over time.

If your email open rate was lower than previous emails to the same subscribers, you might want to test a different email subject line if the email is part of an autoresponder sequence and will be sent again to other subscribers in future.

Almost all email systems allow you to "split test" email subject lines by randomly selecting one of two (or more) different emails to send to each subscriber. You can then measure the different open and click-through rates for the different variants. Ideally you should also use a different link in each email that allows you to measure differences in sales too.

You can do the same if the issue seems to be with your email body and call to action. Keep the subject line the same, but vary the body copy and/or call to action and use that in the split test. Again, measuring the differences in sales (or other goals) is your ultimate test.

For testing your opt-in forms, you can use tools like Google Analytics Content Experiments, Visual Website Optimizer or Optimizely which will let you randomly show different opt-in forms to website visitors and measure which ones get the highest opt-in rate.

If you have a relatively short sales cycle for your products or services (for example if most purchases happen in the first month after people become subscribers) then rather than just testing for the best opt-in rate you can also tag subscribers and see which form results in subscribers with the most sales.

Measuring, testing and improving your opt-in forms and emails can seem technically challenging when you're just starting out. But if you get going with the basics first: just using your email marketing system to test different subject lines for example, it will give you confidence to try more complex tests. Once you start testing regularly it can lead to major improvements in the results you get from email marketing.

Summary

Sales are the ultimate measure of effectiveness for your emails. But you can use more detailed measures such as sales per subscriber and subscriber growth to track the overall health of your email marketing.

To measure the effectiveness of individual emails or opt-in forms, you need to test them under "controlled" conditions. Most email systems allow you to send two or more different emails to random segments of subscribers to see which one gets the best results.

Your Next Steps

- Create a simple email dashboard with overall sales, sales per subscriber, subscriber numbers/growth and sales per buyer and buyer numbers/growth. Monitor this monthly as a measure of the heath of your email system.

- Check the split testing capabilities of your email marketing system. Split test subject lines and calls to action in any important emails you'll be sending out repeatedly, such as sales focused emails in autoresponder sequences.

10 EMAIL MARKETING TECHNOLOGY

So far I've rarely mentioned any specific technology or systems for email marketing. Partly that's because almost all the strategies and techniques we've looked at can be implemented on any email marketing system. And partly it's because, like all technology, specific email marketing systems are updated with new features fairly frequently. However it's worth looking at the different *types* of system you can get and who they're the most suitable for[21].

Different Types of Email Marketing Systems

- **Basic Email Marketing Systems**

  These systems provide the core email marketing functionality, allowing you to create opt-in forms, broadcast and autoresponder emails, measure statistics and manage subscribers. Pricing is typically in the $20-$40 per month range for a few thousand subscribers. Some of the popular systems include Aweber, MailChimp, iContact, Constant Contact and GetResponse.

- **Integrated Marketing Systems**

  These systems include marketing automation (triggering actions based on subscriber activity) and integrate other online marketing tools typically needed by small to medium sized businesses: shopping carts, membership sites, landing

---

[21] Thanks to Jason Mlicki of marketing agency Rattleback for these definitions.

page design, affiliate management and offline marketing (e.g. postcard campaigns). Prices tend to be in the $300-$400 per month region for 10,000+ contacts. The two main systems at this level are Infusionsoft and Ontraport.

- **High End Marketing Automation Systems**

    These systems are designed for larger organisations and include more advanced automation and integration with other corporate systems like Salesforce.com for CRM. They tend to be geared up for more users of the system with different roles (e.g. having specific views for marketing people vs. salespeople). Pricing for these systems is usually $1,000 plus per month. Some of the popular high-end systems include Hubspot, Marketo, Silverpop and Eloqua.

For most readers of this book, the place to start is with one of the basic systems. In fact many quite large organisations still use these systems to manage tens or even hundreds of thousands of subscribers. My advice would be to test out some of the most popular systems to see which one you get on best with. Each system has its advocates and whether you like it seems to be a very personal decision based on how well the workflow and usability of the system "clicks" with you.

Make sure you go with one of the mainstream systems as it will make it a lot easier to get advice from experienced users, and to find external tools that work with the system. I know many businesses who've opted for a more obscure email marketing system that seemed like the perfect fit at the time, but when they then tried to use it with external time-saving tools found that the two wouldn't play together.

The time to move up to an integrated system is when you've mastered the core features of email marketing and are looking to do more advanced techniques like list segmentation and triggering actions based on subscriber activity. In addition, if you're trying to integrate multiple systems like email marketing, Customer Relationship Management (CRM), a shopping cart or a membership control system, then it's worth considering an integrated marketing system that can take over many of those functions and simplify the integration.

But don't run before you can walk. Starting off with an advanced system can leave you spending more time trying to figure out how to make the system work than you spend on doing email marketing itself.

Tools to Make Email Marketing Quicker and More Effective

Some email marketing tasks are time consuming and challenging for non-techies. In particular, creating effective landing pages and opt-in forms and placing them on your website can be very difficult. All the email marketing systems give you tools for creating opt-in forms, but these can often look quite amateurish.

If you use the popular content management system Wordpress to run your website then there are a number of themes like Optimizepress which include built in options for creating landing pages and attractive opt-in forms for many of the most popular email marketing systems.

And you can also get page building tools like LeadPages which allow you to create effective landing pages based on standard templates in just a few minutes and integrate them with the main email marketing system.

Finally, there are tools like Hybrid-Connect and OptinSkin which are plugins that work with most Wordpress themes to allow you to create attractive opt-in forms and place them automatically on your web pages, below blog posts, in sidebars, etc. The latest version of Optimizepress also includes a plugin version to allow it's landing pages to be used with any other theme.

Figure 18 A typical opt-in form created using Aweber (left) vs. one created using a tool like Hybrid-Connect (right)

Pricing for these tools varies from a one-off price of about $50 for some, up to $200 per year for others. But given the amount of time you can save and the increase in the number of opt-ins you get as a result, it's usually an investment with a huge payoff.

If you register for the bonus material for this book at www.emailpersuasion.com/bonuses you'll find a number of up-to-date reviews and recommendations for email marketing systems and tools.

Summary

There are different levels of sophistication in email marketing systems. Most small businesses will start off using a basic email marketing system and may never need to move from there. Other businesses who need more advanced features like shopping carts, membership sites and marketing automation may need to upgrade to an Integrated System.

When choosing a system make sure it's compatible with some of the tools available to speed up email marketing, particularly landing page and opt-in form builders.

Your Next Steps

- If you haven't yet selected an email marketing system to work with, start with one of the basic systems like GetResponse or Aweber. Read the more detailed, up-to-date reviews on the Email Persuasion website.

- Switching email systems takes a lot of work and can be very disruptive to your business. So make sure you really need the additional features before upgrading.

- Review the latest add on tools such as landing page and opt-in form builders. These can save you a huge amount of time and produce a much more professional form than you could do yourself. Check the latest recommended tools in the members area on the Email Persuasion website at http://www.emailpersuasion.com.

11 YOUR NEXT STEPS

Back at the start of this book I told you that email was *the* most powerful marketing tool. I hope that through this book you've come not only to agree on how effective it can be, but also to see that it's something that every business, large or small, can succeed with. If you have something valuable to say to your prospects and customers, you can get that message across simply and with impact using email marketing.

If you're not doing email marketing at all right now then you can be up and running with an account on one of the basic systems and have created an opt-in form and welcome emails within a few hours.

It'll take you a further few hours of thinking and writing or recording to create your lead magnet. And then a few more to write a handful of initial emails for a start-up sequence.

You can incorporate the more advanced email marketing strategies over time as you get more experienced, start getting results, and start to see what works well for you. Iteration and continuous improvement are the key to long term success with email marketing. Don't try to get everything perfect at once. Implement the basics, learn from it, improve, and move on to the next level.

How to Implement What You've Learned in Email Persuasion

Your first step, if you haven't done so already, is to register for the free bonus videos, templates and other material for this book at www.emailpersuasion.com/bonuses. You'll get access to the extra training resources, the latest information on email marketing tools and technologies as they evolve, and the private Facebook group where you can ask questions to me and the Email Persuasion community.

Next, review your current email marketing activities to see where you should start to make improvements:

➤ Have you set clear goals for what you're trying to achieve with email marketing? If not, review the material in the Introduction.

➤ Have you developed personas for your ideal clients and mapped out their goals, aspiration, problems and challenges, and the things they need to know and feel before being ready to hire you? If not, review chapter 1: Winning Clients With Email.

➤ Have you created an initial sequence of 6-12 emails for new subscribers which will establish your credibility, build trust, and which leads them via calls to action to your primary goal? If not, read chapter 6 on email sequences, then chapters 3-5 on writing individual emails and calls to action.

By the way, you can carry out all the above steps before investing in an email marketing system.

➤ Have you created effective landing pages and opt-in forms and placed them strategically to get subscribers for your emails? If not, read chapter 2: Sign Me Up.

> ➤ Are your email subscribers taking the actions you want them to take? If not, read chapter 5: Buy Me, chapter 8: Persuading With Email and chapter 9: Measuring and Testing Your Email Marketing.

Work your way through this short checklist to ensure your email marketing addresses all these core elements and you'll have something in place that surpasses the vast majority of your competitors. And you'll start seeing the results quickly.

If you'd like more detailed advice with step-by-step video training in each of the elements covered by this book, then you can also sign up for my Email Marketing Mastery online training course. It covers every element we've touched on in depth, and includes personal one-to-one support from me as you work through the course. You can get details of the course and a special bonus offer specifically for Email Persuasion buyers at www.ianbrodie.com/emmbonus.

For those who want more specialist resources, I also recommend three other courses on email marketing.

Ben Settle's **Email Players Newsletter** is a master class on writing regular, personality-rich, conversational emails. Ben teaches how to write daily emails that pack a punch and entertain your readers (and repel people not in your "tribe"). His printed newsletter gives regular tips and in-depth insights on using this style of email marketing. You can sign up for his regular emails to check out his unique style and find out about the Email Players newsletter at http://www.bensettle.com.

Andre Chaperon is the go-to guy when it comes to writing autoresponders. He uses a combination of list segmentation along with story-based email sequences to quickly build a powerful bond with subscribers. His Autoresponder Madness course will take you from creating personas to storyboarding sequences of emails and segmenting your subscribers based on their interests and using spin-off sequences. You can find out more about the course here:

http://www.mindvalleyinsights.com/email-marketing/autoresponder-madness

And finally, the very best information on writing sales focused emails and sales email sequences is Daniel Levis's Email Alchemy. I've mentioned Daniel a few times in this book and his course goes into depth into the use of classic storytelling to build a real emotional response to very sales focused emails. You can get Email Alchemy here:

http://www.daniellevis.com/EA_backdoor.html

Most important of all, whether you buy my or other people's courses or you just run with what you've learned in Email Persuasion: **take action**. Get your basic email system up and running with a landing page and opt-in form, and your initial "start-up" emails. Use what you learn from that to keep improving your emails and keep getting better results.

Try it. It works.

And do email me with your results or to ask for advice. I answer all emails to ian@ianbrodie.com personally and I'd love to hear about your successes implementing the lessons from this book.

ABOUT THE AUTHOR

Ian Brodie works with consultants, coaches and other professionals to help them attract and win more clients. He teaches them how to market effectively, how to become seen as leaders in their field, and how to nurture relationships and win business through email marketing.

He was recently named as one of the "Top 50 Global Thought Leaders in Marketing and Sales" by Top Sales World magazine, and one of the "Top 25 Global Influencers in Sales and Sales Management" by OpenView Labs. Salesforce.com picked him as one of their "Social Business Dream Team" and Raintoday.com named his website as one of the "Resources of the Decade" for Professional Services Marketing.

He lives in Cheshire in the UK with his wonderful and understanding wife Kathy who put up with him agonising over this book, and their two fantastic kids Chris and Robs. He's a long-suffering Newcastle United supporter and in his spare time he likes to practice and perform close-up magic (though not very well).

After working his socks off building a consulting business that depended on his personal involvement and effort to win new clients, he discovered that through email marketing he could reach and help more people, have more impact, and win a lot more business. He's personally used the strategies he outlines in this book to grow his own and his clients' businesses. And if you follow these strategies, you can do the same.

If you want to get more of Ian's strategies on attracting and winning clients you can grab a copy of his short report "5 Simple Marketing Tweaks That Will Get You More Clients" here: http://www.ianbrodie.com/5tweaks.

Index

A

Autoresponders
    advantages, 95
    example, 100
    options, 96
    planning a sequence, 98

B

Bnonn Tennant, 24, 66, 69
Bonuses, x
Brian Carroll, vii
Buying an email list, 13

C

Call to action, 72
Chris Brogan, ix
Conversational emails, 67

D

Daniel Levis, 72, 84, 88
Danny Iny, 24, 66, 71, 74
Dashboard for email marketing, 120
Derek Halpern, 33
Double opt-in, 46
Dov Gordon, 66, 110
Dr Robert Cialdini, 112
Drayton Bird, 66

E

Email campaigns, 87
Email design, 57, 68
Email marketing systems, 127
Engagement, 63
Entertaining with emails, 69
Eugene Schwartz, 110
Expert interview, 27

F

Follow up, vi
Frequency, 60
    impact on calls to action, 82

G

Gary Bencivenga, 50
Getting your emails opened, 48

H

Hard teaching in emails, 86
Human interest, 70

J

John Caples, 10

K

Ken McCarthy, 4
Kevin Hillstrom, 120
Kristina Mand-Lakhiani, 72

L

Landing Pages, 28
    examples, 29, 30
Laura Roeder, 40
Lead Magnet, 21
    examples, 24
    first speed bump approach, 23
    how to create, 22
List segmentation, 103
    engagement based segmentation, 105
    increasing response, 106
    interest based segmentation, 104

M

Marie Forleo, 32
Measuring and testing, 122
MindValley, 72, 74, 122

O

One-to-one calls, 91

P

Peep Laja, 32
Permission
    adding to your list without
        permission, 15
    should you buy an email list, 13
    the right way to get subscribers, 17
Personas
    "know and feel" factors, 7
    Customer Insight Mapping, 4
    demographics, 5
    example, 8
    external targets, 5
    ideal client persona, 2
    internal goals and challenges, 6
    process for creating, 2
    the power of personas, 11
Persuasion
    authority, 116
    clear and effective communication,
        111
    commitment and consistency, 114
    liking, 115
    motivation, 110
    persuasion tools, 112
    reciprocity, 112
    scarcity, 117

social proof, 113
Popups, 34
Preparing subscribers to buy, 79
Productivity tools, 129

S

Selling in emails, 83
Sender reputation, 49
Single opt-in, 46
Social proof, 39, 113
Spam
    getting through to the inbox, 43
Steve Gordon, 66
Story based emails, 70
Structuring emails
    the AIDA formula, 76
Subject lines, 50
    benefits, 51
    curiosity, 52
    headline formula, 53

T

Technology, 127
The "Opt-in Formula", 19
    friction, 27
    incentive, 21
    risk, 38
    value, 20
Timing, 58
Traffic, 18
Triggering action, 81

W

Webinars, 89

9162047R00092

Made in the USA
San Bernardino, CA
05 March 2014